Alane Rollings was born in Savannah, Georgia, and educated at Bryn Mawr College and the University of Chicago, where she taught creative writing for years. She was married for 44 years to author Richard Stern. Alane has published five preview volumes of poetry. She presently resides in Jacksonville, Florida.

For David Spicer
For Edward Hirsch

For Richard Stern, always
For David Bevington, always

Alane Rollings

REVERSIBLE WORLD

AUSTIN MACAULEY PUBLISHERS™

LONDON • CAMBRIDGE • NEW YORK • SHARJAH

Ordering Information
Quantity sales: Special discounts are available on quantity purchases by corporations, associations, and others. For details, contact the publisher at the address below.

Publisher's Cataloging-in-Publication data
Rollings, Alane
Reversible World

ISBN 9781645361985 (Paperback)
ISBN 9781643788760 (Hardback)
ISBN 9781638295761 (ePub e-book)
ISBN 9781638298908 (Audiobook)

Library of Congress Control Number: 2022913141

www.austinmacauley.com/us

First Published 2022
Austin Macauley Publishers LLC
40 Wall Street, 33rd Floor, Suite 3302
New York, NY 10005
USA

mail-usa@austinmacauley.com
+1 (646) 5125767

Table of Contents

Part I

Reversible World

But little time will be left me to ponder my destiny! The circles rapidly
grow small—we are plunging madly within the grasp of the whirlpool…
Oh, God! And—going down!
—Edgar Alan Poe, Message in a Bottle

Multiply me by a billion and say I have orders from God.
I don't understand them; I've sworn on my life to uphold them.
I'm honored to have some heroes with me
On this grand venture for the sake of Earth.
Since mythic times when we intertwined with beasts,
Signs of doom kept came from the sky: *Earth's in critical condition.*

How goes it, soldiers? Tell us it was worth it as you gasp your last.
Ours was the usual past: A wronged world, wronged again,
Wronging everyone, but all so long ago, we didn't know it anymore.
I've seen the Leaning Tower, the Pyramids, and the Coliseum,
And been proven worthy of attention from a master painter.
I lived with him for many seasons—10 years every night.

When we opened up the past, we saw that human wishes,
Often past impossible, often had been granted.
Why shouldn't they be?
We'd kissed the elms, moved by frost upon them.
We knew the planet's mood swings. We didn't take them hard;
We knew their necessity to let her cycle on.

We saw her wounds heal quickly.
Back then, there was no hurry.

Statues stood 2,000 years in castles, changed hands every year,
Stayed grand. We miss our heroes; exist because of them.
Must my husband rest 10,000 years in a ceramic urn?
Five years ago, or it may have been five hundred,

We studied lost cultures and wars for free will.
Were the continents playfields? Wheels reverse;
We can fix them—like loaded dice which died in Pompeii,
Which lay near a crater piled, like hell's gate, with ocher Sulphur.
That was news for a journalist like me.
I've swung over to the last place; I'm expected.

I'm a trekker in the farthest Northern reaches. Multiply me
By a million. A crack in the purity of ice becomes a lake.
Cracks appear by billions. The ice won't hold my company.
I cross alone; others follow. We're thirsty; can't drink ice.
Break a dam; water falls: Furious walls. We try not to die.
If the ice were a painting, it would be a masterpiece.

Forgive me: I didn't see mountains exploding
Black smoke while Nero set Rome blazing.
Alaska melts; California burns. Evolution's basics:
Mistakes; Recapitulation. Rome's dreams were born again.
Yes! Backtrack! Backtrack! We haven't come too far
Since the last 'great dying' to a time of mastery
And the honor to advise over 3 billion souls, scared; sorry;
With good moods, bad moods, inscrutable moves.
We'll campaign for the planet. Were we born to be deceived
That our heroes' statues are less dead than we?
Can wheeling wheels reverse? I have no faith
In *world without end, Amen.* We hear of nuclear winters;

Comet winters; hopeless populations, relocated to temperate zones.
   Multiply me by a billion self-deluded, disobedient souls
Facing death-threats. We seek solutions to renewing history.
   Come back, come back, you ancient, blooming heroes
Who neither live nor die but are convincing when you try.
   With your voices in our heads, we must go back
And never say goodbye to the Euphrates and the Nile.
   Ice is melting on a tundra shrouded in a frozen dark.
   But it's been a good day, and a glacier makes its seaward trip:
A thousand miles.
   I carry in my heart that man, my lost husband, who weighs as much
As an idea—and is as immortal. He weighs as much as an eternity.

   Call him what you like. Multiply him! No illusions!
   New World, have a grand day!
   We are the Resurrection in a temple we've bedecked
with Japanese prayer slips.

Two Grains of Courage

My business is going on. People asked me how to go on,
and I counseled them while wondering how I went on and barely
kept myself from begging them how to go on.

—Toni Morrison, *The Bluest Eye*

It's a darker dark now.
That outer dark with terror: No return from where
sentences skid into emptiness.
I'm a fragile parakeet, caged in one small room
where a tiger's entered: *One more blow; I'm gone.*

If I were Pythagoras, I'd have a theory that worked.
It was a ghost, but his belief in it gave it reality.
He had a way of thinking God could share, and he got away with it.
I've counted all my life. I have a T-square, L-square, slide-rule.
I think: *If I count to seven and the phone doesn't ring, I won't die today.*

But thinking like my life solves no riddles.
I think: *If the postman comes by noon, I'll live through the year.*
But that's merely half a chance; I can't forget the other half.
I think: *What time is it in Tokyo? With the difference in time zones, I suffocate*
Myself with the unknown. Blood, a high-pitched chirp—smashes at my
Eardrums.

My punishment, connected to no crime,
Is evidence: I'm unnecessary. No one shares the vertigo
Of my uncertain future. I think: *If my apple has no spots,*

I won't get cancer. But the far wall slides away, the door within it
Bends, then the adjoining walls ebb off. The ceiling peels away,
Sucking air out of my lungs. My body bucks in shock.

Then a whisper creeps onto my tongue, bleeding, pleading:
Spirit, Fly to town! Abandon what's just slammed around—my heart:
A canary in a cage. No one needs my language skills, my wounding dialogue,
And infatuated cravings.

I say: *I have my mind. I'll invent another life. It need not inspire.*
I'll reveal my killing anguish.
That disaster which caves in my head is mine. The beat of pain—the beat
Of pulse—throbs: D*espair's your biggest part. Study it!*
My senses, strung to concert pitch,

sound chords at breaths of wind. All I know fits on a razor's edge.
I'll dislodge the bird-bones of my words stuck in my throat.
Then a robin, a brilliant singer, knocks himself unconscious
On my bedroom window. His aloneness separates each being.
Words alone—coins collected from deep cracks—

Touch my thoughts, penetrate this abhorrent darkness.
Two syllables cry out to the wind that wheels away.
I stretch. My muscles sing. Rivulets of strain pulse through my arms.
My head falls back, sees the world, reversed.

I know why David wrote Psalm 23: Pain.
I know why God, with a universe to run, shaped two fists of flesh
Into 100 billion nerve cells, names it 'human brain.'
He didn't have to let a sparrow sing.
It was His idea to replace my confidence with shives of fear—shrapnel

In my head. His idea to let my heart stand tests; thirst for goodness.
A baby bird, wings extended at 100 feet to a life that waits
Behind a fringe of leaves, grows intent upon a sky alive inside his mind.

I gather my two grains of courage, flap my arms, limp in circles.
Circling is as much God's plan as phrases which hold meaning.

On some non-descript page of non-ruled paper,
I print, with my slant, conversations with myself. My sentences flow
Past paralysis to where life waits. I ache to walk into it.
St. Francis knew of trouble. It has its way with us; love's inseparable
From suffering; despair implies some solace. I am not my wounds.

Like a dogwood with its crosses, I have faith my phrases may stay safe.
The miracle: *Beauty*—a robin who flies freely—offers me
Another day of desperation, with its streams of kindness.
These waken me to all the little prisoners who see me, need me,
Who are vulnerable, like me. We stand on yearning's ledges.

Each light is good; the word 'sweet' enters me.
My hands give me what I need to make myself anew.
My daze hasn't thickened; it's my vision, quickening
To solve, on a napkin, a mathematical proof.
I see that, since the universe came to be in a moment—

Infinitely small, a single point—everything's its center.
The center of the universe—a lulling, city dove,
Sits, like me, at the speed
With which we reach the future.
We can do no less or more.

Passerines

It's good news—couldn't be better unless God plotted it.
It includes universal parallelograms and correspondences
Of the moods and eons.

Doesn't crystal split by its own laws? And calls of chickadees
Resemble spectrum patterns of a violin, from which the sounds of clarinets
Vary only slightly? Communities of crickets hum: A benign continuum.
Our footsteps match our heartbeats. None of these cut tracks in consciousness;
They dig deep in old ones. The song of one heart, broken, sings for all.

Whitecaps roar and fall. If I were a cloud, surveying islands,
I'd see the spokes of bridges over worn-out coasts
And walls of kudzu climbing their tall pines.
When the riverbank wakes, seagulls speak.
The scent is wood smoke. The morning fog's so thick,
It cloaks opposing banks, makes the river seem a sea.
I fight my way up-water; the wind kicks at me,
Keeps me pressing inward. I turn each turn again.

Time has set the rhythm of existence.
God's a reference to decipherable patterns—distant weather systems;
Whitecaps' rise and fall. The world's a mountain with crevasses open wide
Beneath deceptive snow piled in its cornices. These beauties join larger ones:
A multi-colored scene, with black hawthorn's emerald leaves,
Purple-thorned choke-cherry, and skin-colored eucalyptus, split to crows' calls.
The rocks' 100 shades of deep-scarred gray, Earth's foundation,
Has been ground to tiny shards.

The past tense has come quickly of its own accord. Remembering
Every spring—in solitude and pounding prayer—cracks the heart for life.
   Our blood sinks softly in the riverbeds of dreams; separates us
From our darlings. Wind claws air. Water batters us, to thunder-riots
Sharp as teeth that bite our skin then tumble to the undertow.
   Gray wisps of cloud form skulls that glare into our souls—as novel
And as old as roadside cliffs. They can't conceal despair for Earth.

   I'm a doubtful traveler on a beach, gazing, not yet setting off
To sea. Light streams from every quarter of the sky.
I embrace regret, longing, and whatever else lets the world flood in.
My words, unspoken, rustle through me like blown leaves.
My eyes gnaw at their sockets; my spine gnaws at my hips.
   God chose me for quick shifts while Earth vanishes—
A green bug on a branch.

   Love says we must love hope,
Which bolts off—a frightened gull. It's still love for us we witness.
We converse with bulrushes; call ourselves prophets; fend off the high water.
   A hand at my back gives a push; I let the breezes take me, let music
Bathe me. Sometimes, I talk to doves, domes, and birds of Paradise
In Hanging Gardens of Babylon. Among tiled roofs and chanters eager
To be elsewhere, we cling.

   I hear prayers, whispered in the past by lovers and the old.
   In cyclones of hurt and hope, they lean this way and that, like us.
   They've wept so much they've turned, like Phaethon's sisters, into
willows.
   Time no longer flows ahead, but between us, parallel, a looping string
That doubles everything. Sad scents of honeysuckle, thick-as-mist wisteria,
And long white lines of ships, wobbling in water, waiting for departure to a
Sea with no shortcuts. Blue as undersides of mallards' wings, it's Nature's
essence—

Harmonious as snowflakes. Calls of egrets make our speech unworthy.

Still, we speak. To the sea which owns the traveler; to boats whose holds
Have barrels where events are jammed.

It's a long meander to the sea. I'm one of Baudelaire's thousand voyagers,
Scarred but waiting at eternal foothills to read shapes of cumulus; read Time
By the angle of my shadow—for the sea to be hard as the agates of past
kingdoms.
I'll ride my ship, a carved Pallas Athena, gazing at the Future.

We'll rise through blue obscurity and shift in peril on a disc of ocean
Which represents the globe. I'm a passerine, poised for flight, ready to take
Off, leaning on the wind. Blessed connectedness lets the ocean take me, fast;
Breathy. where she was going anyway: The next to cross every next horizon.

Sister Prisoner

I've been here before, looking at her naked,
Looking at her looking out for me.

    Heaven's too far overhead. I can't detect its shadow
Even in the errant moonlight. It's as if the sister light
Has slipped inside me, breathing, *Be invisible*. I stare at space,
Exhausted by a weak commitment to my life; backlit by each new moon;
by time's embrace of me; by your embrace; by mine of you.
Every night the Sister Light offers passage to the next.

    My sister prisoner's been awake all night,
Flaunting her full halo, her purity of babies' tears.
    We'd like to wrap the night, vast and careless, around us;
We need dark as well as light for clarity; reassurance
That the sky won't fall. Nothing shines until it borrows light.
No one but the sun lets her sister be a crescent, lolling on her side.
We know why prisoners love her: her continual efforts
To escape the clouds. She moves; we move, too.

    When lightning strikes, the sister prisoner ignites,
Plunges to the friendliness of the infinite sea. It flashes green,
Proving what a small moon can achieve. She brightens highways
Into yellow ribbons, turns deserts into inns for sleeping gypsies
Undisturbed by nudging lions. Why should any sky fall on us lovers?
    It's not my style to promise moon and stars, but any minute
Ragged clouds might shaft the black-gum trees, leaving undersides
Of leaves ruffled pale and fragile in a quickly gathered dusk.

We all implicate ourselves, time after time, in crimes
Against humanity. Earth is our slip-sliding game, with stage-sets
And reflections of our shadows. They sift like salt through our numb fingers.
Pearly frogs chirrup and fine, white froth breezes into reeds
The prisoner light's made blue.
We go on loving one another; our sister keeps on suffering
Through trials, rounded by the sleep of her invisibility.
Underneath black trapezoids, furious clouds rush in to further block her.

Yet, her shine's a passage back to the shine before—on more of life.
Tonight, we may see less of her, her silver mast on our gold battleship.
When she comes back, we check on her, seeing if she's moved. She *has*. Have
we?
She's the one with time to spare. She summons, with sympathy,
The planet's ancient glory: *Earth, you're not too old to be more beautiful!*
You and I call each other *baby.* Moonlight covers, then reveals us lovers.
When we stare at *you*, Sister Moon, lovingly enough,
We're transported, by osmosis, into a chastened prayer at a temple we can't
touch.

Nor can clouds that fly past you, nor can the sun you can obscure,
Completely block you out. You send shadows walking on the grass—
My Love's is taller than all others. Under rooflines you have specked with
shine,
We reflect your heavens to be reflected in them.
We don't plead to meteor showers, splattering the sky
Like a Pollock. *Isn't heaven watching out for us?*
We beg our sister, *Extra light!* And keep loving one another.
We embrace her who embraces us, unsparing with frigidity.

Confess to crimes against the planet? How can we not be on courses
We love each other! The sky has not caved in!
The moon rises golden, swollen, open-hearted. Triangulated
By a steeple, she throws shadows of fig-branches, curled like hands
Into our hands. They turn us inside out: Turn fretting earth,
With her moth-white gardenia blooms, upside down in rescue.

In sympathy for us, the moon doesn't linger in her rounded mirror.
> She lets stars let us listen to ourselves. She's more worn out than we.
> I've told her we were on our way, brave as babies.
> With light-lace—her mercy—she parts the sky's dark waves.
> Into high bright air, with our celestial escort, her-blank, all-seeing eyes,
We rise toward bruise-colored night, a basket hung from stars,
And gaze, souls consoled, at tadpoles in a murky creek.

The Way Forth Is Back

As we look out, we're also looking backwards,
Toward the point of singularity.

—Neil Turak

What if instead of evening news, someone threw an x-ray switch
To show the world at its worst: a photographic negative?
Dark and death are what we'd see—corpses rushing toward
bombed homes on bomb-shelter subways, two heartbeats too late.
Streets: War-zones; back-slaps: Stabs.
Laughter: A machine-gun ratatat tat. Cries for help—*I'm hanging*
by my toes! Stand for final human chains.

No rescue by the world. The landscape shakes in crackling,
Orange flames, poisoned smoke floats over, ashes fall like baby powder.
Was home ever anything but violent? Weren't, we always ambushed
By its unpredictability, left alone on someone's whim?
Things go awry as quickly as a cracked track flips a train.
Bombs sleep beneath our feet; eat them at a misstep;
Burst churches open into bone-deep decimated hope.

Artful lighting makes inhumane dilemmas—
Where will we warehouse mental cases?—seem merely unsolved.
Newscasts puncture public narratives—*no one's poisoning*
The water —with hypnotic radiance.
It pours into and out of us; it superpowers towns
Into swarming insect Hells with trusting people shrieking, *Don't let go!*
We created theories that are lacking.

And we were God's best notion!
Life sprang out of His imagination!
Despite wars and climate horrors,
We thought Him our ally. Life renewed itself through history.
Timetables made our trains derail.
We squashed the teachings of the times earth tilted.
Dust bowls provoked cirrus-wisps into dripping acid.

Trains are fire-breathing dragons
Whose screeching made us weep—not tears but small, black stones
Which burned our eyes that made them.
Soothsayers in Dante's Hell stroll—heads twisted back—
To show that God alone foretells the future. It comes disguised;
If it came naked, we'd be petrified. Attached to it, we rush; try to catch up—
To inhabit our grandiose hopes for it.

Everything clings with flaming fingers.
Will we over-handle fragile hope?
Time and Love, each a Proteus, shape-shift.
Time's an elastic band, Love a forgiving puppy. When stupid fingers
Pull the world apart, resident angels put it back, stronger.
Prayers work as hard as hands. *Ah, History!*
The ancients thought it wheeled and turned its million spokes a day,

So swiftly no one understood it.
It's a wonder there was any room for the womb of time
To love the Earth to birth. New, we go by heaven's ancient lights.
Cries for help flail in air exhausted, always bearing cries.
We roast in violence against our silent selves; in opinions' ovens;
In news of large and little fires we fan while trying to put them out.
Is God playing with us, lifting hopes He'll kill?

Every time we walk with our eyes skyward,
He proves our vision's perfect unreliability.
Look back! Nature reached the windows in the Renaissance!
Classic earth and human glories, rediscovered with their wisdom,

Out-did Medieval pessimism.

Leonardo, hardly an original, re-invented tanks; cannons; catapults;

Rescued the idea of man, proportioned in a circle. What next—or what before?

Look further back!

With nagging humanity, the Arabs reclaimed Aristotle:

I have all measures in me. divine ones, and those to come from Earth to hell.

Ever missed a train? If we could stop and gaze around,

We'd be puppies seeing color.

God has not corrected the idea we're more important.

We can't see time and love move forward.

Look back further! See a crunch of Titans—Neuron stars!

It generates precious matter: Waves and light.

Conflict sparks Creation. And dreams from our imaginations:

Consolation, freedom, havens.

So, we're mid-revolution?

The future is too far ahead to tell.

But there are repeated miracles anyone can kiss:

A million seeds, bulbs, roots, weevils, hurricanes, and birds,

Recurrent losses and recurrent hopes of a reversal,

For jumps into the infinite

By trains on endless trestles, wheeled by our souls, spitting sparks.

Dead Ahead

I think about the end of the world all day.
Stricken, I kneel, and my desperation lessens—or increases.
    The sky turns around, and I bless my luck
At having lived long enough to have been intimate
With sun-showers. I trace history to a first cause.
    From its blood-thickened plots, I untangle threads
Matted by the weaving daughters of inevitability. I'll see
How the arrangement, like tiers of air and Earth,
Is constantly reworked—to a new disarray.

    I ride the ocean, rocking like a coffin.
    If we believe we see ourselves within some future dream,
And make a few adjustments, we may lose it.
    An empire loved by a quadrillion people
Could be pulverized, its citizens plunge through portals
Into interplanetary dust. Why should history then begin
To tell us a straight story? We seem to live in it;
It lives in us. As if inside a stream, winding forth
And back around itself, we will ourselves ahead.

    Some—whose vision will admit
Only the corrupted past, say, *Don't dream! Some things
Shouldn't even be imagined!* We who think
We're people of the future, say, *It's time. It's time.*
    We adore the magnanimity
Of the unborn. Our cause: To insure it's just the future
Dead ahead. We call, *Look out!* Life answers,

What's the point of preaching courage to the trapped?
     A devastation-rattle accompanies events like 9/11

In our panicked, hammering hearts—
Which burst again at endless acts of sacrifice and kindness—
An honor to the race. *What next?*
     Leap. Back a century. To the Titanic—
Too death-draped for imaginings, beforehand or afterward.
As usual, God and nature gave us a time being:
     We did not dispute being called dreamers,
Duped, at times, by illusions of sea-worthiness,
Though nothing actual met our expectations.

     What we knew: *Time is infinitely looping.*
     We moved fast in freezing sea spray.
We had leaders on our luxury liner. Though they
discussed with us no grave responsibilities.
     At some point, we realized we were sinking
And trampled one another while the wireless failed.
The heroes of those hours had read the ghostly crowd—
For whom they sacrificed themselves. *Come back!*
     Failing that, another leap, back, back three centuries.

     How goes the world? A blur that seems reality.
     Science took time past our senses.
     Newton's gravity passed all the tests of non-existence.
     Darwin called us kin; claimed nature tricked to death
Her most distinguished children: The world's largest butterfly
And Galileo, dying blind and lonely.
     To fathom Evolution, which brought us here
Against all odds, despite all motives, mixed appallingly,
And all ends unpredictable, leap back, back, back!

     The first cell was fertilized, as the planet cooled,
By a lightning bolt. The microbes invented sex;
Swapped energy; caught electrons,

Strung them into infinite loops,
Exchanged DNA, created species. Some buy this
Only if we humans sit atop the 'ladder to perfection.'

     You'd think, to hear great nations think, they're
The only ones who count. No end is predictable,
Yet they step out saluting *History's Beauty*.
     They mock the revolutionaries who broke rules
And marveled at small violations in the law of physics:
The unaccountable spokes that stick in Saturn's rings.
Others love defeats of noble causes. Why learn from history?
     We say, *one function of a dream: Wake us up!*
     Darwin's favorite book: *Paradise Lost.*
     Evolution is a truer story, it selects for optimism.
     April, 1914: The engine room flooded.

     Power lost, no wireless.
     Our heroes: *People first!* Some jumped railings!
     Possessions never! We had to join each other;
No food, no water, compass, chart.
     Lights blazed under waves.
     Yet, on the listing ship, a five-man orchestra
As sublime as God's outstretched hand, offered
Stony woes and steps to heaven,
               Nearer God to Thee. Aye, aye.

Like Thunderbolts

Though I've forgotten how to act with saints,
I talk to Jude, the patron saint of desperate causes.
I could use another saint.
    My brain locks when I talk; my heart slams
Like a canary's cage. I clutch my stomach, labor on
In diffidence, given life's insistent snubs.
    When rationality's too strange, the surreal takes over.

You woo the future, spurn the centuries gone by,
Propitiate a fickle, enigmatic lover—Life.
    I'm sentenced to life-long confusion, accompanied
By inner music; I did not compose. I drag mysteries behind me
In puffs of sunlight, glinting from the pavement, in air
Ferocious as a hurricane.
    In my head, action slows to a dream-like glide,
Frame by frame, toward contradiction's quicksand.
    Then, I see a movement of your hand
Fall into eternity: a gorgeous cricket from a stem.
    The rational transforms itself to nothing grand,
Just a sturdy structure. It may or may not break
Beneath the weight of ideas, longings, terrors,
And, in days by the yearnful, the world's cruel shocks.

You define our lives as precious moments in the mind.
    The mind! That it might contain God's purpose
And the goading questions of the Universe!
    Could we believe in God and ask nothing of Him
But to let us stretch like thunderbolts and shout, *Oh! Oh!*
    Given Nature's bombast, I have a sense
Of culminating tragedy. Fitful bits of funeral verses spill
From my lips, do not add up.
    I've got this daily dialogue with God.
    I say, *May I stop now?*
    God: *You're against Nature? No! Keep ducking*
Through the mental battery you make
With your parody of faith!
    You: *No lovers' leaps into the universe for us!*

    Longing's called 'longing' since it stretches to time's end,
At the mercy of past history and the clatter
Of the world. It lives on thresholds: Life's; death's.
    God: Unstudied love is not a means, but a purpose.
    It lies in life's web of symbol, omen, coincidence,
And sly, benevolent Providence with its trails of tears and spit—
Sub-atomic to galactic.

    But there's no limit to my intimate shame,
Which brings more shame, though I recite psalms in my sleep.
    Your shining phrases float past me on wreaths of smoke.
    Clouds lift like gates; red lights glow through
Like your dazzling theories of our starts and ends.
    I was born with arms too weak
To reach the sky, with dust in my mouth day after day.

    You sing for the past, then turn your gaze futureward,
Backstroke toward cascades! You create ideas
Which refer to what we cannot see, hear, grasp.
That should be enough. Yet I let the world tilt, slide
From its foundation, call it my fall, call you too perfect

For God to let you go. You: *Why say we've reached our limit?*
    Spirits don't die; they improvise, modify, extend.
    Everything in sight hums: *Eternal life!*
    The number of melodies is infinite.
The sky's no limit, and it pours the universe into us.
It's life, not death, that has no limits! Light can't end…
The universe splits: To infinite universes. There's glory
Just in sitting, an abundance past imagining.
You sing out majestically from the world's wreck,

    We'll run our fingers down our backs—
Like Doubting Thomas across the palm of Christ.
Nothing dies like us. But spirit, sanctified, lives within
Your blood. Pain may pulse, yet sweetness wrenches
In our chests, holds us bold as thunderbolts.

Open the Charts

Open them! The maps of heaven and humans
Haven't changed since ancient Greece.
    Earth's a garden in the mid-space sea.
Each century's new; air, cool and brilliant.
The famous sunrise goes right on, stirs wonder—
Palpable but hidden in each day—
At the earth's survival and at ours.

    You and I, our planet-hope as bendable as tin,
Pretend we're upright, though we're flattened
By a brain-deep disappointment in our governments.
    Once we flew above mediocre heads.
    I could not match your arcs and swoops.
    You leapt, eagle-like, between gold branches.
Our hearts beat a beat apart but with a constant bassline.

    My hand upon your head, you played long piano notes.
We rediscovered man's grand invention: The kiss.
    Your shoulders squared off, met the rest of you.
    To compute your mathematical proportions,
I took up, with a compass, Greek statuary. I copied
Leonardo's bodies, played with Dürer's triangles.
The mathematical theories that rule particles and galaxies

Govern human life. Let that go on, too.
    Woods—God's first churches—shimmer now like skeletons.
    Words—which teach beatitudes and ecstasies—bubble
In us like white water, spiraling like interstellar space and DNA.

It took ninety generations for environment and genes
To produce your brain's billion switching elements.
     You're just the man to open up *The Book of the Pearl Planet*—
Within the tender arms of spiral galaxies, within the swaying universe.
     You question heaven. Might its age, size, and composition
Tell us how our bodies met and swerved toward happiness—
Feathers on a berried branch—with harmony as magic as the spheres'?
     We bottled our embraces for ourselves in fragile cases
Of our bones. Your body recalled everything; you could push
Past its complaints. It knew how to unveil; to leap. Your hand

Upon my head lets your pulse sing thin and fast inside my head:
Heaven's current coursing through.
     Though just a touch of fingertips, I won't let it go.
When I draw circles on your chest, it vibrates—a piano
With the pedal down. My shivering hands open
By the same electric impulses as in between the stars.
The moon, a lamp, your skin: Stars with an increasingly small radius.

     Through all the stardust that careens
Through space, you pick up Jupiter with your transistor.
     But we break, bit by bit; lose blood and bone
While standing up. Yet your chest against my back
Is my happiness! My gaze stays in yours. Such blue-gray eyes!
     Such answers in them! Bodies of heaven, bodies of Earth,
We take our blood-warm forms unto each other, beating, beating, love,

Surging toward each other as if about to burst, as if loving anything, anyone
Means loving Earth; wishing its persistence.
     Our bodies keep changing their minds. *Am I ill? Are you well?*
     But the length of a foot measures a foot. I can step it out
On my kitchen floor.
     The force that moves Heaven moves us—
Though pain may well become the beat of pulse.

Earth's Jupiter and Venus are in worse shape than our flesh.

A pain in your arm moves to your shoulder, your back, then to the center
Of the square inside your circle: A universal ideal form. The stars look down
As if, like us, they would revive the dying chords
Of orchestras of Earth and sky.

Part II

Dungaree Doll

Once he fixed his eyes on mine, how could I help what I saw?
　　We stared, and the past refocused, clear as glass
With the complex stillness of summer afternoons.
　　I'd drifted in my opiated, memories, glanced up, and there he was,
The gold thread through everything. I pressed his hand and heaven rushed
Between.

　　Despite my soul's back alleys, we shared a mind as primary as the color
'red.'
　　He had hands of a pianist, incandescent as if dipped in milk.
His black piano opened: An enormous heart. He hit high C's, sang to me,
Dungaree Doll, my Dungaree Doll, Paint your initials on my jeans!
I leaned over him, made his singing linger.

　　I loved his face, lined deep as his days. We felt twenty, lilacs after winter.
　　I pulled him close, willed his strength to seep through me.
His love burst open in me like a *paw paw*.
　　I vanished in his eyes, the color of the shallow Caribbean.
　　In a sky pale as an old nail, he could tell the time within ten minutes.

To within ten minutes—with a despairing quality, as if he'd seen
Our eventual fates. He mourned when grief for someone else
Refused me a reprieve. Without him, I couldn't even whimper.
　　A comma of blond-white hair fell across his eyes,
But when my name slipped from his mouth, I wrote his on my palm,

Affirmed that brilliant, dazing, shattering, delicious thing: Gratitude for being.
That swell of happiness had to happen. We'd met at every concert:
Streams that burst around a fountain, pooled again. His voice, a star-shard
With the lusciousness of honeycomb, lifted in a sweeping run of notes,
Competing with Keats' nightingale to seduce the delicacy from silence:

Keep twisting my heartstrings, sing the bells of Saint Martin's;
Oranges and lemons, sing the bells of Saint Clements…

I'd known white-hot blinding heartache.
Yet I loved his passion, all its aspects. If I were an angel, I'd pity me,
Who loves so much love's wound imbued with bliss.

He wraps me in Debussy, Gershwin, sweetness:
His initials on my jeans.

Visible Transfigurations

With hearts sore-pained within us
And our brains' basements flooded with desire, wild as blue clouds
Of sorrow, in sacramental light, in unfathomable dark,
We eat raw sunlight. You and I fling our days behind us.
    But let's begin with weather, dirty weather
With its threatening undertone of wind. It whistles through
Our old ship's rigging with a woman's mournful whine.

    Mountains rock and roll to the ocean,
And the drunken rain, buffeting, resembles windful waves
Which shred our sails and tear them off our masts.
    Our boat lies on her beam; both sides groaning.
    In these moments, life's dailiness is altered:
We've found a place for a transfiguration.
    It's as if a chasm opened, and a pit angled from the planet,

Whose white trees glow like ghosts. Silver snowflakes tumble
To a gorge: *Down. Down. Lost.* Then, no sign or clue remains.
    We need a panorama to meet the panorama
Of the continuum: Something to enlarge the soul until it feels
No need for mastery. Only for a garden where enlightenment begins.
    I imagine I hear whispers from years past:

Husbands' ghosts riding on the currents of the air
While tunes emerge from hiding in the pockets of their clothes.
    Come on, Teacher, make some notes for an extravaganza.
    Form them as originals of nature: Hardly of this world.
    Let tiny snowflakes blur the scene

Like an impressionist painting, where nothing seems
Real enough to touch.

     Let our silhouettes upon the ridges
Be substantiated into human figures.
     When dancing starts, we'll stay close to our partners,
Fit in all our steps. The northern lights will glide away
In their impossible shades.
     When God first entered, He gave drama to the Arctic:
The drama that's repeated in our lives:

The harrowing uncertainty of love.
     He created angels, who could show Him splendor,
Then the fissions, fusions, comets' tails. Then He made you. And your viola.
     Then, a hundred thousand snow geese,
Wheeling, banking, flaring in a unison which sings
That Nature is the show—with her outbreaks of aurorae
And electric storms—that will never end.

     There's one glory in the sun; one in moon and stars;
Another in the ocean which we ride.
     God made you with a flick of His fingers.
     Your sky bound music spread by His injunction.
     We use Him as a reference to undeciphered patterns.
     Years create us: We end too many days.
Yet every time you play, it moves me more and more.

     You play until you cry, soak your viola—
It might occur at Lourdes.
     You're a fingerprint of God. Your music
Connects us to the cosmos.
     The great performances of glaciers unfold.
A sheer drop at the top, then there's a band
Of pointillist silver, gleaming like the sea.

     I trace the heart's far tracts, quickstep

My joy and hurt without a word. All the future that I need
Is here. I won't ask if there's time for it.
    Why would I say I've reached my limit?
    I train flashes of remembrance on your face:
Hidden spotlights. Time skips half a beat
As if it's dozing, then wakens in a snap.
    Who wouldn't wish to witness the universal dance:
The visible transfigurations which refashion us?
    You pencil notes on snowy composition paper
With the faith Beethoven had in melodies he found in his deaf ears.
You carry on the dance of soul and science.
    Calliope, goddess of music and dance
Whispers in our ears: *Look! Listen!*

    Grasped by tilting light, we keep seeking revelations;
Visible transfigurations. Love has entered. No intoxicated sweetness
Can compare. First, it's a dart into the eyes. It moves on
Through the blood, makes us blush. Our pulses rush
As if breaking through our skin. The calls of snow geese,
Joining ours, fly together, arcing upward.
God is entering, once again, our picture.

A Page of Time

From the stillness of paralysis, my legs move.
    Walking fast feels good, as if a miracle is happening within me.
    The morning light upon my steps races off
As if to say, *The Earth won't die today.*
    I'm crazy for Nature: Cedars' colors pulse like yellow flames;
Palmettos rattle—dancing bones—through tupelos;
They're God's marionettes. I burst with hope
For a reversal for our *mater* Nature.

    I think of my worst day: My husband's death.
I saw that morning coming. It bore down—a brakeless
18-wheeler. I spent months in continual wind;
Blown sand smashed my windowpanes.
    I repeated, *Good old Heart, don't forget to beat!*
It's that beat that keeps me running in the silence barely pierced
By early stirrings and small quicksteps of my parakeets.
    In the evanescent present, I feel the future's pull

Upon the ponderous past. Of the three, I can't say
What I have least of: Each is made of moments,
Given, bled away, then quickly vanished in a sunny, timeless void.
    Like nature, I take orders from the sky.
    Wind-tears streak my cheeks. Within the angle
In between my ribs and shoulders, I don't just love: I persist
In love so thoroughly, I've earned a thousand candles
On my birthday cake.

Like all of nature's children, I bear the scars of time.
They make me restore myself—
And help cleanse her poisoned streams, her plastic dumps.
And help our polar bears.
Every day I say, *It's a holy day. I'll say Amen, then say
Amen again.* My precious parakeets, in dewy-breath peace,
Sigh *Why?* I answer, *Because it's all the souls of my beloveds
I address. When cousins touch my hair, make me aware*

of their hard lives, they alter what I am. But being a romantic
is my calling; I could accept no other.
When downpour softens Earth, perennials shoot through
Soil, and I look forward. *To look forward—*
Such a simple act. Serene as an unrippled stream
In a vista with the wonder of a space waiting to be filled
Again with good old world. I lean into it at a slant,
Arms outstretched like a bedraggled, cross-less Jesus.

He was a page of time that altered Time's next pages.
Oh, for such a teacher now, to reach into the interval
Between Earth's start and finish, and fill the pure luxury
Of *Now* with the sun's hot honey of replenishment.
He'd keep us all from being turned to gas and poured
Into the stratosphere. He'd let us say, *Sweet Jesus, let each day
Be like this one!* If only our intentions were contained
In the phrase, *Hope of life.* For one tenth of a second—an eternity—

All flapping wings would pause and time would reconsider,
In mid-flight, its course. Now, the summer glare is heady
With orange blooms, with buds of tangy fruit
Curled beneath them. *Jesus, will you release the oranges
This year?* That suspense is a challenge: To create our future selves.
We're people of the future, *in* the future.
Yet, in our daily dusk-dawn marathon, we haven't
Thought enough of it. Since we don't take care of nature,

She won't spare us, though she's our stone
And hasn't slipped mid-stream. The bark of beeches
May be dove-wing white. But melting glaciers, racing
From the Poles, bear down on us.
    On the edge of vast potential, a ceremonial phrase
Is frozen: *Nature's sick*. Let her pummel us!
    Time can't be commanded to make Jesus bless our days,
But when it lurches forward, it seems to love the future,
As we do. I wake in the middle of the night

To the sound of no-sound: The future is waiting. I ache
To walk into it and keep its microclimate mild, autumnal,
Welcoming. *Love of Earth* is contained in the words *I love*.
    But I don't think. I feel. I'm weak as a stream,
Dizzy from collages of expert decisions which flow
Out of bodies, windows, doors. Darkness flies to darkness
With the birdsongs from wavering leaves.
    In the yellow drift of another waning year of paralysis,
We're here.
    While sunset burns itself away in reds slashed with gray,
A moment loops around us. It turns us, and, in our hands,
It turns. It's this recurring page of time:
Hereafter's Here and Now.

To Hold a Dreamcatcher

Aphrodite used the Little Dipper to scatter magic through open windows.

I embrace a child to enfold myself in the future.
To live is nothing but to love; to bare one's soul.
Blood's more precious than rubies,
Which my girl is worth. Blood is us: A pool of life,
Dispersed in us. But it belongs to nature. It's not given,
Only held in trust. I see it in protruding veins. It seems to live in me;

In fact, I live by it. When I regress to childhood, I get another nosebleed.
I smell the blood, taste the rust of it. At ten, I couldn't guess
How the world should change, though it had entered me like blood.
I drank from one cup, one day to another. I saw more in others
Than they saw in themselves, prayed for everyone, to justify my life.
I never had a baby. I claimed a spit-shined little girl, Eliza—

A refugee who'd crossed, alone, armed boundaries in Africa.
I drilled a hole in a wall, installed a toggle-bolt to hold a dreamcatcher.
This protected her from nightmares as she slept. Good dreams,
Slipping through its opening, got caught and held within its feathers.
Now she holds her dreams like hope. Her heart beats to mines
We're allowed to be happy. We never sever touch or imagine death.

Though I use too much space, breathe too much air,
The pull of possibility unwinds between us potently. I'm no one in her absence.
Lost is lonely. But she's with me, even when my voice is a white noise in my
head.
My chest aches and swells; I hope my bones won't crack.

My vulnerability has lodged in her.
The crucial rules? Love and comfort flow ahead; God keeps

Firm eyes on us all. But do I have a plan?
Peacekeepers dig wells, set up nurseries; kick around
Old soccer balls; clean rubble off of little souls.
They smile and carry on. Prayers—for the families who don't know
What's happened to them—recite themselves in their heads.
How can I understand this blazing anguish?

And the presences of 10-year-olds like my Eliza? Everywhere, their eyes!
I say, *follow me to life; we'll hold hands for peace.*
I pray, in all denominations, for my girl—until I hurt.
Like wind and rain, we cling. The shower-pattern
Seems a slowing heartbeat; sounds like loss. A fairy-tale gate-guard,
I'd thought all boundaries limitless; I have limits now.

My bravado hides a tremor. I pray to a different moon each night.
Eliza is awake, darkness in her face, picking at her sheets as if to keep alive.
She knows what happened. Her village burned, displacing children
To terrain as broken as a barbarous theology.
She was grateful for the dust on windows: It obscured the scene.
Altars exploded; roofs collapsed. In the heat shadows sculpted,

Her eyes lit with despair. Pots clanged with the sound of church bells.
The space between her shoulders shifted, locked.
The land was melting, oozing brown saliva which dried
And crumbled into dust. Chaos. Crowds. Streets: Living, sweating
Dragons of humanity, inching forward, wheezing dirt, honking horns.
I tore action from myself to ease her disaster, her secrets, fears, wants:

They lived beside my own; her chin jerked beneath my hand.
Her voice was soft as speaking underwater. I shared
Her ragamuffin speech—*I want; I need.* Our voices pooled in blood-soaked covers
And in memory's amber. I wrapped her soul around me.

I told her; *I'll stay. I'll read our every sound and silence.*
Aphrodite cuts the air with her bare breasts, frightens people

With her urgency; doesn't say a word, but sees meaning in us all.
She lifts, without a sigh, the world's whole weight of love.
    Earth needs her—and me.
    I telephone authorities all day. My heart's a fierce red cup,
Tucked among quicksteps, giggle fits, and the name I've given her—*Eliza*—
Clutched within my fist. She rises, bringing rhymes: *Ladybug, Ladybug,*

Fly away home. Your house is on fire; your children will burn.
    Dry earth swallows blood. The art of ages, bombed again, has vanished;
Love and blood flow forward. We hang on with straining hands, solid with
God.
    Come away, human child. Your mind has no matter.
    But songs are us; ideas are us; blood is us: The blood of others
In the common light of cries; of moral issues old as scriptures.

You know what caught dreams you hold!

The Bloom and Shine of Spirit

God can be a louse.
    I woke up. My hot dawg was gone, solid gone.
He took the dump truck. I'd smugly held him, a bottle of milk
Spoiled sour. You know how peach tree-roots can curl so deep,
They freeze? Then, no peaches.
    One dude offered drugs to speed up time, another,
Drugs to slow it down. Oh, I'd lost days. I could take

Being gotten wrong. I said, *I'm just fine*;
That was just the lie I had to buy. I'd gone blank
Before, hand-cracked my legs to push on forth,
My lungs, to take another gasp of my inane present
Of humidity, garbage smells, brown streets full
Of brown dirt, brown souls, and ailanthus trees
Full-leafy; brown forlorn.

    In the small-souled darkness of the house,
Omens lightning-struck my strobe-lit brain. I plunged
Into revulsion and a drenching nausea
At the writhing ugliness of trust. Even folks I envied
Seemed dark peaches like my Squeeze, moldy to the pit.
Grief was scramble-egging me.
    When peach trees bud, their fruits can bloom.

    My *whatchamajigger* was the one who knew enough
To freak out with me when the porch's shadow slipped
And swallowed the front yard. Now my mouth
Hangs out—a window, north wind whipping through.

My re-organizing steps get wrecked by drafty, nasty
Rafters, reliably collapsed. *Oh, I thought he was hi-class.*
My eyes, he said, burned through his feet, even when
Screwed shut. My good red blood that revved his pulse
Would fill a beer mug, free of charge. Muffled city uproar
Dampens and defeats my dirty winter heart. Clock-hands—
10 till 10—say time's about run out.
     I jump to dodge a close-by house; it might fall down.
In night-time dark as asphalt, peach shoots poke
Brown stitches through the brown ice of the lawn.

     Blacktop doesn't blaze a trail;
West wind gives no direction. How to renovate
My digs to a forever-dwelling?
I feed the 'keets pecan bits, corn meal to geraniums.
     The doorbell rings; I smooth the wrinkles
From my skirt, shake my numb, heavy legs—
My little homewrecker's come back!

     I let my brain knock loose and flap—erratic,
Like a bat—through my skull's empty halls.
     On small rat-feet, a monstrous meltdown
Skitters up my spine. What great payment
This time? *Whoo, Boy! You slap-happy Rabbit!*
     What great payment will it take to reinstate me,
Let me show a winning hand to God?

     The shades snap up: An axe-sound;
A welcome to a soul upon a threshold.
     With a flashlight in the dark,
We'll check the goldened backyard blooms.
    But the monstrosities and the murderous days,
How do we endure them, how do we take them?
                         —We praise.
            —Rainer Maria Rilke's

Down the Gangplank up the Ramp

Depending on the weather, I suffered hideously
Or was blessed by challenges to soul and intellect.
   We were a frieze of men and beasts, configured like atomic particles—
Various but dangerous from envy, hatred, and suspicion, all invisible.
   Enemy number one—the sun—was what we craved. God let us live that
way,
Each of us with properties—limbs' labor; writing's slant—to which no one
else had rights.
   We sniffed air; inched toward waterholes; retreated; turned 'round on
   ourselves.
We women remained mute to men's mayhem. Me, I'd been had—and named
the cad.

   Gluttons craving victory over unpredictability, we lived
As if living were no sick and fearful treachery. We bit like kids and beat our
chests.
   Pythons ate gazelles who couldn't match them breath for breath;
Hyenas scarfed the grass that zebra blood had gushed upon;
Rhinos beat the ground like drums. Though recently emerged from an ocean
of deceits,
We didn't see our beast-brains where our human secrets spring. We lay
Our crimes against each other at the Devil's door. We went to school
And shot out street lights. We were decent people.

   We'd heard of men who chanted kill-lists and burned houses down.
In any glimpse of any one, there was a share of dark.
   God dogged all our steps. We were fit for love or nothing.
   In my dream, we were the beasts, two by two up to the ark to safety.

I narrowed down my enemies to one Spanish pirate-
Mongoose to my mouse. In his dreams, people shamed him, as they did everyone.
He began a trick on me that went on in his absence—
A blaze refreshed with fantasies of fire.
    Do we have to kill each other? Even ocean tore up light when it
        encroached,
But ospreys had decided how they might divide the sky. Why keep seeing
Differences in similarities? Shameful conflicts floated off unsolved. Killers slept at night.
    While parakeets banged heads and feet, leap-frogs sang antiphony,
And goldfish clicked their teeth, the people we'd depend upon gazed across the sea.
    They saw stained-glass martyrs: Abraham, Rosa Parks—sacrificial lambs
Who walked off ships to history—and who'd foreseen that most would not believe them.
That background music—locusts swayed by termite tympani—wasn't it necessity?

    Those meditative runs which reached a pause to re-begin, and to which
We beat our breasts—elegant, redundant tones unaccountable except
As the nuanced speech of biology—weren't they a score for matter's transformation
To a chaos ordered more and more? A love song busy being brought to life?
    Take any nude, group close-up: women look more nude than men.
As a girl, I'd let myself become an artful composition—
Shadowed by the Spanish pirate who had seen his differences from me.
He'd photographed a half-nude girl of seventeen, and kept me in captivity.

    Why pick me? God has us all surrounded, and we women knew
We were unpopular. Our vision quests existed only in our fitful sleep.
Yet in gold, low-angle light, among 100 million skulls of sacrificial victims,
We'd merged with all there was and ever would be.
    My photographer went to extremes. In white-out conditions, breath
Plumed from his lips. His photo of me was a summery escape.
    In shadows formed by legs of men outstretched across my waist,

my open hands gestured, 'Come to me!'

    This high-seas buccaneer was the sole witness of sweet innocence.
    He warned, 'Keep your flesh enslaved by dread.' His stolen gold:
unknown.
His photo wrecked my reputation, pushed me down a gangplank
Overhung by skull and crossbones flag.
    Satisfied with that fifty-year-old photo,
His pirate's face and mustache kept their charm. He sipped spiced rum.
I'd never begged to anyone but God.
    Now, I talked a pirate into generosity.
Why feed my greedy heart to sharks?
    What would let me hold my fair head high,
Pushed to strength in robes of dignity, in buoyancy, broken-
A trance—out of the sea? Reassurance of my privacy. Safety!
    Thank you, Lord—no one had more to use against me!
    Words are fire. Words are light. I called his bluff,
Again spoke up. Cheetahs scratch their coats over all their rattling bones.
I moaned, *let me be! Set me free!*

    God dogged our steps. The pirate yielded
A little victory: He released me. Anybody could believe it:
We'd been pressing, men and women, toward moments of agreement—
A movement in a ceaseless symphony—*oh, do, Lord, shine through me!*

Ring in the Nobler Modes

Ring in the nobler modes of life
With sweeter manners, nobler laws…

—Alfred, Lord Tennyson, "In Memoriam"

Head up, with quiet hands like a princess,
Evie's in a lovely daydream. She's thirteen. A prince, lace at his collar,
Would sing, *Come away!* at an alabaster fountain.
Life moved toward her. She'd stride, guided
By intuition's light, and know her course
Would toss up obstacles she'd hurdle.

When she had charity in her soul for herself,
She envisioned her future, inviolable life, no harrowing dawns.
A pomegranate, her heart burst in gratitude,
A fruit split open to reveal a thousand seeds.
Morning after morning, she felt cast into life;
Given chances to show her intelligence, her character.

She thought chance her personal assistant, with her power
To implement her imagination. But events sifted
Capriciously through her fingers.
Evie opened herself to the world's nonchalance,
To teen sites on the Net. She chatted with a stranger,
Who claimed he was in high school, then in college. He was thirty-five.

She thought he 'got' her. She was armed
With eighth grade biology and the expectation of a decent world.

Whoever he was—all registered sex offenders matched his profile—
He ran a ghost program, paid cash for motel rooms
And his airport rental Chevy.

Her weapons now: Quiet thoughts of his beauty.
Why would a virgin touch a pervert?
What happened in the motel? The man tricked her, promised
To massage her feet so she'd lie down. Her blood ran through his fingers.
After the rape, she was sure he loved her, was more beautiful
Than other men. Evie made a desperate assumption:
Someone was tending lights at ends of tunnels.

To her, common sense was the voices of a million
Truthful ghosts. What's believable was unforeseen.
Her best friend snitched on her, took her to the hospital
In the red bra and panties the rapist gave her to wear in the motel—
And a pink trench coat. Two thousand fresh rape kits in the freezer,
And Counselor Annie urged, *Let the misery slide off of you.*

Just let it go. Evie, a woman with a history now, but little present life,
Responded, *I can't just start talking like Tony Soprano!*
It seemed to her the rape hadn't happened, or that she'd watched it.
He'd texted, U lonely 2? I'm looking for a young sad girl
To train. She posed for him in the red underwear.
She said he never forced himself on her—they'd made love.
He was John Doe; he'd emailed her a photo of his penis.

He posted pictures of her naked.
The detectives began at the motel, then to his website.
She hoped she was more than people saw; could be even more.
She wanted help for the poor, beloved, anonymous rapist.
Evie wrapped herself in her innocence, an aspect of her trust,
Thinking was a lonely, painful job.

Annie showed her pictures of his other girls.
She was not the only lonely one.

She'd rather have been poisoned than sanely learn life's strict limits.
Her body had betrayed her mind, quiet as a stopped clock.
Now, her heart seemed to slow; heavy blood trudged in her veins.
He'd trampled anger into her head with cowboy boots.

His whispers crept up her throat on tiptoe, stabbed her tongue.
She squeezed her breasts as rushed confusion moved through,
Then out of her head. Tires screeched; horns honked.
She gasped at the white pigeons in the park, so glorious they hurt.
What a miracle that birds emerged! There might yet
Be joy in thought! Dragged by the arms like Tantalus,

She finally felt thirsty, with cool water near. She thought, *Dear Inner Self,*
Let me be of use. Nothing happened from hesitation, but she hoped
Her fresh, unsparing measuring of herself would keep her soul alive
'Till she forgot what she was trying to forget.
A winter cipher, arms around herself,
She pressed her helpless charge against a more elusive cypher.

God Shots

There are ghosts we so believe in, they're real:
The laws of physics; gravity. On rare, smog-free nights,
Stars are glimmers of a shimmering immensity. They seem signs
Of a benign, even benevolent design—in which the cosmos forms
From chaos. My terror: I might not return
From my life sentence here on Earth, but slide beneath
A patched sky to emptiness.

    I'd crawled into grief's tormented music, cocooned it
Around me with the sharp scent of fear, and with my dead,
From whom I felt no different. Like mine, their trapped voices
Were amplified by solitude. They made the walls around me screech
Like strangled doves. I'd spent the morning sweating, muttering curses
At decrepitude. The room tore their noise apart.

    Did people leave especially me? Every time I heard
One word—*good*—I loved my dead more. At my door,
I stared into the sky—a dark, horrid thing, heading my way
In tense quietude, as suspenseful as a held breath. Above
The charcoal clouds, over lanes dark as caves, over landscapes
Black as ink, and ominous, there hovered Purgatory's ashen,

Incomprehensible faces. Dead leaves skidded across
Filthy sidewalks; crows haggled on telephone lines. I felt
Awakened from a coma to a world radically changed.
    I understood the saying: Man plans; God laughs.
Panic lurked just past my field of vision, stalking, sure to pounce.

Yet I made one last gamble on the tug of irresponsible events.
    I had no more room inside me for the slow, inward bleeding
Of despair. I had a hair of hope—a God Shot—for a miraculous reversal.
    Still I, who'd slaved over all the Great Books,
Regretted each new breath, as if optimism were a weakness;
As if belief in hope meant I must cling to that alone.
    I asked God how much longer Earth

Would enfold me in ravens' wings. In place of promises or threats,
I'd take a sign that symbolized transition. Transition would be no stranger
Than any poem I wrote with a borrowed pen—*une plume*—
On white pages *au clair de la lune*...
    Then a thousand words flowed forth. They created lovely images
Of the spreading horse-chestnut trees on the Champs Elysée.

    Dramas turn on reversals. Misdirection is misinterpreted,
Driving lovers apart, antagonists together.
In romance, the distance between true loves decreases.
    It creates a bower of earth's purple thickets, vine-looped timbers,
And cascading scents of jasmine, tulips, and tuberoses.
    Every substance has its weight, which holds

Tremendous energy. That's the power encased in rocks, ducks, streams,
Communities of parakeets and crickets, and dove-white birch tree bark.
    Each day, I choose a moment—fast, before it passed,
Since a soul changes quicker than the sky—to let some grace
Enter my pale skin. Such a God Shot gives me strength
To carry on.

    It could come in the form of a line from a book:
A bright, blank canvas on which I could paint a fresh narrative
About my life...It could be an image from a film: A tiny
Violinist, making her wood sing...astonished, I realized
These players, from whose words and scenes I make scriptures,
Are dead. They'd been eternal students, as I am.

None of us were authors of autobiographies.
    But God Shots, with magic logic, made the world make sense again,
As good as we had made it the day God kissed our eyes.
    I'd fallen, gotten up more, certain of my faith in nature.
She's capable of thought; of joy. Her every death's a seed;
Even her droughts bear plum trees, par *l'amour de Dieu…*

    The northern lights pop with Pentecostal sparks,
And, at the cathedral, pigeons bring me 3000-year-old songs.
    From outside God's shut door, they give me back my soul.
My eyelids droop. I'm a grounded dove, intent on unseen skies;
Blessing heaven for hard life. *Mes amis, my candle's died;*
I've no more fire; my door is open wide…

Part III

Ice in the Ocean

In this rugged blue and white corner of the globe,
All the disappearing life feels as close as the frost-smoke of our breath.
    What is sacred? What is spirit?
    In peripheral vision, in slanted sun, the Arctic's frozen and detached.
    When ice turns into water, is it bliss?
    Something lethal's taken root,
A poison tree whose drops have poisoned all the streams
Of a race in overdrive, urged top-speed toward money.

    A phrase—*hope of life*—wafts over from a distance,
Echoes through gray clouds, then floats through gray confusion:
A rough diamond tossed out like a prayer to a God we hope exists.
    From our Lilliputian souls, which shine, hideously,
Through drowsy flesh, we ask, *must we give birth to death?*
    It's easy to project: People, aging, crawling, beating
Weeks submissive. Ideas race back and forth:
Science, politics, religion.

    You and I sit, as if poured, in easy chairs, untouched
By spirit's icy, urging voice: *Complete your projects!*
    What's worth living for?
    We thought nature was made of inseparables:
Men and gods; life and hope: drops, dropped together
In jade oceans. We knew what she could do, that she used us
To get herself remade; that she hated our abuse.

Caribou paw at ice; they know something's wrong. Blue leaves

Turn inward and hang limp, as if grieving. Water climbs water cliffs
To crest, gasp, crash. Lashing, smashing waves,
Exceeding any fortress walls, meet the mistress fluent
In *only if's*: the sea. Gray, she meets gray air. Heavy ripples,
Drifting nowhere, like our movements, make us think all action
Sinks to nothingness.
     We stomp the caribou, who press their hooves
Beneath their limbs, from bright cold into dark.

They'd known the voice of roses that had breathed
On their white Eden. They didn't think the world heard.
Their tormented voices tell us we're still living,
In a space where *the impossible* is *possible*.
     Call it an invisible trapdoor, a placeholder
For our memory, which holds Earth's events
And catastrophes to come.
     Eskimos call us whites *the people who change Nature—*

From a placid ice-scape to a murderous vortex.
     Floe by floe, snow unfolds, seems solid.
Then, a giant swell, hidden by ice-bridges,
Which flowed fast beneath us, splits it to a myriad crevasses.
     An ice column, bright and tall, rises in our faces,
An airy, smiling angel of death.
     Warmed, glaciers, held in place by ice-shelves,
Get unblocked, thaw, flow ocean-ward.

     Half of Greenland's crystal pavement,
Once cemented by the breath of Neptune, has melted.
     We dodge the subject of death: The passing
of Eskimo curlews, Labrador Ducks, Pallas Cormorants…
     Polar Bears, seeking ice to rest on, drown.
     Like light, Time's a passing beast, hovering, hawk-like,
Over tundras or collapsing like a penguin, heart-attacked.

The long light lets you and me sit with history,

A pebble we turn over in our hands. The land knows
We've been there, bringing iced despair. We've traversed
The haunting exhalations of a herd of caribou. We've gazed upon
The breath-trail of a gliding albatross who's outlasted wind.
    Rearrange this place!
    The land climbs inside of us.
    What's worth dying for? We clench our teeth
So, we won't shatter—bits of snow in water.

    See how melted ice lifts the sea,
Turning like a dragon in half-sleep! Reverse it!
    Reverse the stupefaction which has set us sliding
Off the steep horizon of our consciousness!
    Faltering doves of promise,
We traverse crevasse upon crevasse, silence inside silence.
    How long will we live?
How long hear the frozen gasps of those with ice inside?

Days Without Sunrise

While I thought I was learning how to live,
   I was learning how to die.

—Leonardo da Vinci

   Close to Poles, winter passes ceaselessly in seasonless glare.
The air vibrates with the majestic urgency of melting.
The cold slows respiration; we press our lips together in hard lines
And watch for floods. Fires, flowing ice.
   There's something of original creation here.
   In the dissipating stillness, time pools like water.
   You and I sleep on tundra with no sunrise.

   Glaciers rise above us: Great white ships
That tower over oceans aubergine to lilac. The white ice-scape
Makes me feel we've crossed this stretch forever,
With voices barely audible over snow-melt's roaring rush.
   Our words might as well be tossed to waves
Heading oceanward with broken loads of ice.
   Politics invades this place.

   When madness climbs the throne,
No one escapes contagion. Polar bears, who'd feasted
with muskoxen on inland crowberries, now race
in circles, gnashing their long teeth.
   Our mouths ice up. Our shivering muscles have contracted.
They spasm all night in the mute darkness
Where words bear actions that address our weather.

Your clock whirrs and strikes to Nature's wounds:
Pistol cracks of ice contracting inside thawing glaciers.
Krill recedes, with ice, in toxic algae-tides, letting death
Claim narwhals, penguins, whales.
    We think as clearly as the wild chirps of blackbirds
In black treetops. As clearly as the ocean rises, wave on wave,
Meeting massive mountains of carved ice.

    On these days without sunrise, horizons elude us.
    Kilimanjaro's far-off, vanished snow
Makes me stammer in dismay, keeps you awake
In acid-tasting panic that rends, tears, crashes,
leaves us limp as feed-sacks.
    On days without sunrise, we stand on frozen ocean.
The surface shows no symptoms of our torture of it.

    It's a stationary platform. An orphan, like ice in the ocean.
    Something of creation's here.
    Glaciers, like magnificent, cracked vases,
Have your spirit to re-form.
    The river-ice crackles. Cracks three inches wide
Grow, in seven hours, seven feet across. The high rampart
Of a mesa-berg, sheared smooth as your forehead,

Progresses, implacably, toward ice-blocks.
    They gleam like obsidian and surge up, half a mile,
Gouge adjacent banks. Icicled branches snap and crash
With whining pops at dead gray weather over dead gray dirt.
    Our quiet's shattered further by the whacks
Of cracking, making frightening new cycles in the life of ice.
    Rivers; ice floes; animals; you; me: adrift

In unknown seas. Lights reflected off of ice
Like the steady resolution which may make some headway.
    Oh, unfrozen ocean home! Keep us going!

In icy light reflected by our death-defying lives,
Our Sister Prisoner Moon remains in sight.

The Respiration of Drenched Darlings

All my prayers seem to melt down to one for grace.

—Flannery O'Connor

Thoreau's early walk graced his day.
    I'm rooted, but I study the Tiepolo blue morning sky
To know how night will go: Lonely.
    From my picture window, mist-draped birches
Are pale green—like my Mother's eyes. Their flesh-white bark
And tangerine leaves reflect in estuaries thin as fingers—
Pointing at all angles at a sea with waves that ram, recede.

    As if a wave were worth my dying for,
I clutch my chest and live forever in the thirty seconds
It takes one to crash.
    I write my late Mother's name—*Irma Lee; Irma Lee*—
Again and again. Like nature, whom she was born to enter,
She was Sanctuary. Some vaporous grace pervades them both.
    If I had weather's self-possession, I could catch

The glory of a stream meeting any waterway.
    I've known those too gorgeous not to worship and regret.
    But my mind's too wide. It casts beyond
Earth's and heaven's elementary routines
For treasures so fulfilling they inspire the awe
I should reserve for northern lights, when they perform
And lord it, with unimagined colors, over Earth.

I could have been a spirit. Feelings kept me
A thirsty person, ambitious, and so civilized, I distrusted nature.
      Yet, a recruiter of sublimity, I admired women,
Like my mother, to whose unstudied grace the world
Seemed perfectly disposed. She'd waited—a seabird,
Searching Windward Islands—without despair or urgency,
As if grace were guaranteed.

      In silent swirls of falling leaves, I count clouds
With my umbrella. Raindrops sift through holes in heaven.
They warn me: *You can also fall.* I'm not solid with God.
      I ache, not for the beauty of the past, only for its certainty.
      The world of people dragged me off from home,
But home had held the world. I never praised it—now it's gone.
      I've become a crying child, whose memory makes harsh claims

Upon the present—whose plastic-shrouded narwhals are too threatened.
      Retrospection, like an Escher etching, is transfigured by the glance.
      A desert sweating salt on a planet barbarous from neglect
Can be restored to fuchsia bougainvillea under Persian turquoise skies.
      Mamma told no risqué stories on the Earth—
Only of its perfect matches —a blooming lion's ear mint
With a red-backed sunbird's down-curved beak. Her one delusion:

Earth was good as she. In lingering shock of loss of her,
I see love's worth living for. Nature moves me as a dying child would.
My prayers have melted to a prayer for grace—like Mamma had—for nature.
      I was created in the sacred time-space marriage.
      No one warned me: *What I most had was me.*
My dithering reply: *I'm not a flowering tree.*
      But, like a cedar, I forget myself and reach.

      I see something in its way of growing ceaselessly.
      Dusk deepens to a darkness premature from thunder.
Plovers, grackles, and flycatchers fly—wings and prayers—
From forests, crying, *we don't own our home!*

Like my mother, I, who lack her grace, am one with them,
Whom we both were born to meet. But I've lived and died in books.
Gutless, graceless, I navigate wet, stirring woods, every tree a garden,
Hung with blue vermilion, purple orchids, and green honey creepers
For the lady bugs and tree frogs' music boxes.
    This feast of sustenance is the cathedral which gives placeless grace
An address. Mother Love, which loses substance—like scorched bones in
sun—
Does not evaporate.
    It lives in respiration of drenched darlings—
Living pinpoints, which persist past reason—

God's trillion glances, cast below:
    Yellow buttercups with crickets on their petals,
Waving, *Cousin,*
Get us the forever you don't have.

Oh, Take Us to Your Care

You and I answer calls from subtle, continuous rhythm.
With bell-like sounds, a song begins, then quickens.
We dance to the beat that melody needs.
Tension vibrates from our limbs and tightened mouths.
The first note sounds; our heels tap staccato to the desultory chords of Bach.
He's our dominion's King. You've absorbed and memorized his music.

    I sit up in ecstasy as if to music of the spheres:
Angels ever bright and fair, take, oh take me to your care.
      The smallest moment ruins or redeems.
      These seconds are the precious underlay
Of crucial future memories. They pass in blurs too fast to grasp.
      Unpunctuated hours slip by, flashing to God's stopwatch.

      Shadows dance down walls from diamond desk-lamps.
      The gift of music bathes us by the moment, finds a place inside us
Nothing touches. Our fingertips and feet share the same feelings.
They encase beauty, which envelopes us: a perfect prayer
Even God would not deny. It haunts our eyes and hurls emotion into us:
A madness that becomes a willingness of heart. Your Bach sits astride

Our narrow world. There's no place his glory can't not touch us.
      I make nature-treks through the Bible.
      Cows dance to music even after music stops.
God gave them golden hooves and swallows' grace.
      Their pathetic mewls distil their longing not to be afraid.
Beside them, we converse, our voices hard and sweet as tiny peaches:

Not this one…nor that…not her…not me— and fail to see
The magnitude of a moment's gift.
     Weather moves into your face and your eyes become soft rain;
Your eyebrows bend: Hovering limbs of evergreens.
     Suffering binds us. Nature screams. We'll die for her,
Whose landscapes circle us with silver walls, again and again.

     Snakes curl around every capital letter in the Bible. I'd flee,
But I believe in God. Look into the wind! Surrender to that apparition!
You and I would sacrifice all usual events to a breeze whose every particle
Of sound live and moves. We sleep and wake to new waltz music
And the scrapes and drums of orchestras beneath an ancient laurel tree
Whose green exceeds all emeralds'.

     Storms are different now. A three-degree shift on the thermometer has
Changed their courses, forces, though days progress at the old rate.
     A fast tide of anxiety skims over us. Time's former shape
Hides beneath now's blanket.
     Orpheus turned for one last look at the ghost of his beloved,
And, in that pulsebeat, lost her.

     Time marks our place, then bears us back to our hot womb—
Then our grave—with any moment's sense of the Absolute.
     That begins with this moment, which can't be relived;
Which weighs against a lifetime. We're better for our dance together,
In simplicity, which lets me lose myself in movement; in you.
     Music takes the pain from your wounds, makes even my grief sweet.

Lush, midsummer seconds outside of Time are gone—
Like the green of an apple barely balanced on a branch.
     Time's ocean stretches broad and open.
     No becomes a yes, we won't diminish by a breath—
     Come close, darling moment.
Let us bite your hand.

Ring the Longing Bell

Miracles do not happen in contradiction to nature,
But only in contradiction to what we know of nature.

—St. Augustine

    I've been touched by the impossible;
I've tasted its hot magic. Except for my love's goodness,
I've known no simpler miracle. Either makes a moment
A perfected gift; his kiss, a heart wrench different from all others.
I'd thought my torso was too scarred and gaunt for anyone to want.

    I'd thought my idealism had been buried in a lonely grave
In a nothing little place; thought the world too ludicrous to live in.
I heard the ring of my love's bell of longing, knew why it frightened me.
    Our first fifteen minutes were so far beyond a clock,
They might have lasted seven seconds or a hundred hours.

    He called me the resourceful jay who made worry fly away;
He erased the extra space between us. All we two could do was bow
To the imperative of filling it again—with the euphoria that lived so vividly in
us,
A stethoscope could pick it up. Memory rang our longing bells, then poured,
In heaps, sweet recollections. Each one hurled itself at us: *It's me you want!*

    Given his endearing, heroic disposition,
The lines of his *Ave Marias* swooped and swirled like evening swifts.
They opened my left side and, in my heart, left his bright, insistent voice.
    I was no stranger to the world of feeling, nor unpracticed

In expression. But lifelong chasing of the Everlasting

Left my knees as small as parakeets.' I rang my bell of longing, and exhaustion
Flew away. The peals held the thrill of a frightened nighttime bullfinch,
Protecting family territory. The song sang *love and suffering*
Are so intertwined, by nature, they're the same.
    My love became a series of epistles, written to my love.

I'd never heard the Madrigals he swam in.
    With my stomach taut, stretched and fragile as a rubber band,
He studied me: an Inca Jay, threatened, yet capable of a devotion
He could cultivate. I shook my head, a city woman feeding
unseen pigeons.

    A whimper rose from me. I turned, side to side, shrank back, shook
My head. His eyes were bright; convinced; his posture straight enough
To persuade me, swaying on my feet, to act urgently. I put ten fingers
On his shoulders so I wouldn't shake, and told him,
I'm living all I can: Not enough.

    In the seconds it might take a robin to return from a window
Where she'd banged her head, to her blue eggs' nest, I exchanged pain
For the fierce fledgling love of a soul in wonder.
    He didn't try to be himself; he was he, tender as a goldfish fin;
Sturdy as the Hanging Road which bridges Earth and heaven.

    His arias exceeded a splendid oak's magnanimity.
I wish I'd taught him all he knows of music! He's taught me
How it's born in heads! He knows, like birds, that *song—doubled prayer—*
Means communion. His letters told me of a world where music's rise and fall
Mirrors feelings and defines us.

    Where men, beasts, plants, fish, rocks,
Birds, and Earth remain, by miracle, alive—
    I count upon five fingers the weeks apart from him. I suffer.
That's love's innumerable threads, each one thin as beaten gold,

Interwoven into iron.
We have a home in that stone.

No Outcome's Unforbidden

We watched those B movies: A lost guy spots a spaceship
Come to kidnap one lone earthling. The start guarantees the outcome:
A one-way ticket to the future. There are fixed possibilities,
Yet no outcome's unforbidden by Physics' laws.
    We bought tales of aliens,
Yet did not believe that our nation could be prey.

    Heisenberg said it was impossible to measure
An object's position and speed simultaneously. Uncertainty had spiked.
    Determinism then diminished Will to an illusion.
    Yet, we freely ache for a simplicity of certainty
To match majestic space-time curves. We move in three dimensions;
It's hard to think in four. We can prove the first by walking straight ahead.

    Turn left: That's the second. Up a road, we add the third.
    Where's the fourth?
    Time, which obsesses us, is as demanding as it seems.
    Like everything, it isn't flat or solid, but has holes, wrinkles, voids.
    The faith of Science tells us nature hasn't yet made up her mind.
    But ideas of science get replaced. If we're certain, faith's not faith.

    When matter was a speck, space-time filled all cosmic corners.
    Then the universe was inflated into life, unfurled, unfolded
With a mathematical grace: A cloud of gas, with the disconcerting ease
of innocence.
    Where *is* everyone? We're lonely on our small blue ball
With its oscillating brightness and musical vibration!

Thanks to lack of order, we were born. There are others out there.
    Apple trees are fastened to the Earth and vice versa.
The connection, true as stars' steel points, magnifies each item in clear focus,
As a cricket on a leaf reveals the vein on which it sits.
    Each thinking of another, everyone arrived.
    We'll put a neon sign in space: *Call us!*

    We'd come from nothing to the iridescent Madagascar jacarandas
And black rock as sensually perfect as carved marble.
    Perfection's no more possible than certainty. But nothing
Can make itself impossible—even raging lightning storms on far-off planets.
    The universe gives us birth, then splits into theaters of sunlight.
    The space beyond them has a grace past speech.

    Nothing's lost but may be found if sought: Faith's articulation—pourings
Of symbolic waters; theories lovely, simple, generally correct; the light
Of consciousness of beauty called the soul.
    Time's unlikely to be stuck on us. The comfort of its passing
Is that it falls, like snowflakes—one upon the last until *what is*, is covered.
And that it's coming soon.

When the Universe Bends
Over Backwards

Thou hast turned for me my mourning into dancing: Thou hast put off
My sackcloth, and girded me with gladness.

—Psalm 30

My love was one of God's best men.

We love the poetic realm, which disdains to destroy him.
I cried like an osprey at his kindness.
He consigned me to live through the thin air of grief
For my husband, whose last breath I felt as deeply
As though I'd drawn it myself. My pain crowded out
Everything but the pathetic truth that I lived in a thick, ugly fog
And a silence so raw, that when I swallowed,
I heard my spit as it slid down my throat.

I swore my photos of my lost husband were breathing.
I reimagined all our talks, polished each word like an agate.
Then I shut my eyes. Through the white noise of grief,
My bones still cleaved to my flesh. The apartment
Still echoed with his voice, a long, cat-fur caress.
I had not cheated death, though my heart beat loudly
In the face of the unprotected, undissected, unaccounted for
Wound, shrunk, at times, to pinprick size—a wound nonetheless.

My faith seemed a remnant of another woman's life.
My grief emanated through stone walls, glass windows,
And dark corners I dared not look around.
From the minute my husband died, I was shocked
By the deliberate dissonance of a confused storm of sounds,
In which bits of musical phrases were drowned, then re-emerged,
As light recedes completely, then leaves a place brighter than before.
Look how I won't forget anyone I've loved!

I won't diminish by a sigh the sanctity of love!
My new love's eyes fixed on mine as if they were a text
He was intent on reading. We were two ends of a single thought.
My heart jerked, tumultuous, in his hands. Words were no longer
Impossible birds who flew at my approach. His letters were how
I learned to read again. His blue words on white pages bore sound
And shades into my flesh. We had conversations in breaths
Taken in, let out. God had given him the fingers and the blue

Of Fra Angelico and the touch and doves of Saint Francis.
We knit our lives together, drop-stitches and all.
I was pulled to him as to air when I was underwater.
His hand beneath my chin held me up to breathe. My strongest
Longing was to hear his footsteps crunch my driveway's ice.
My blood stopped at the touch of his hand on my cheek.
He filled our empty space with words: Tiny, white blossoms
Which dropped like bits of lace on a dressmaker's floor.

His name arched up like hands in prayer.
He nestled close and made my face a book open at two pages:
'Faith' and 'Grace.' I placed my hand in the hollow of his stomach;
It rose and fell as if it rested on a summer sea, whose tide
Came in with a transition sigh. A source-less voice emerged
From the dark, where the ragged heaven-tree fretted, mourned,
Then silenced, down to the tiniest blackbird. The universe
Bent over backward, and I found my love in Orion's belt.

Willow fronds whispered to themselves. They floated,
Hundreds at a time, on a breeze as soft as a baby's soles.
    In the silent haze of reverence, God made us feel less small.
    I nodded ten times to the east, and thanked Him,
My mouth trembling, that I could sip the rain on my love's face,
And smell the white-blond comma of his hair upon his forehead
In the unbearable comfort of proximity.
    Now, he, in whose hand my heart beats, is in fiery pain.

    Now, he takes my arm to keep his balance.
He's bearing the world's hurt. When his fever peaks,
It's the only thing we know. His pain wrings my soul.
    Yet fever makes things magical. It makes winter turn around
A room in sunrays darting from white lances onto silver crosses
On reflective windows. It shows how light connects us,
Like the Brahms my love played on his viola.

    He, who holds me when I need to hold him,
And, when I let him go, releases me, whispers, *There, there* to me.
    His fever melts the snow before his door.
    He puts his index finger on my lips—to hush my fear.
    Miracles are down by half; we only need the one that's he.
    There, there.
    The pigeons in the park are cooing in despair.

The Sweetness of the
Lute's Top String

A little boy was born—my nephew—a small, amazed face
On our lives' edge. Wrapped in a cotton blanket,
He lent the room a transient, makeshift light.
    In lulls of wind, came a cacophony of hooting, honking,
Squawking: Graylags and pintail mallards, with tiny, perfect beaks.

    Then came the shrieks of the baby, bent on finding what he held.
    Blood surged through him in a continuous drumline.
    He waked and laughed a hundred times a day.
    Soon he played his kazoo, banged his tambourine.
Pummeled soldier-dolls, flayed books of fairy-tales.

    Underprivileged as a penguin, tossed in the arms
Of impatient expectation, he was a human pinpoint,
Always complaining; full of hope. History had happened, but he couldn't
Know it. He couldn't know his folks when they were young.
    He came to me, his aunt, with fantasies of narwhals;

I told him how it was to be brought up in the past, with snow
And coral reefs. Then, God answered my prayers for peace
With the word *eventually*. But the irrational continued, day on day,
Beneath the shadow world of towering centuries.
    Remembrance flashed me an apparition:

An ageless, watchful muse, arms bent to cradle babies.
    To help another grow like that! It's love in its purest form!

With a fire in his head, he dove for Earth's last pink pearls
In green, torch-lit water.
    Every day, he titled the day: *Best of All Possible.*
    He couldn't see himself in the eyes of the man he'd become,
Though the truths in his face were as visible as starfish at low tide.
    As if he'd imbibed the world's wisdom
With his mother's pale blue milk, everything astonished him,
Especially himself. He'd come suddenly upon his heart

With its own damnable mystery, its flakes of drifting fear.
    Winter filled his lungs; they babbled and rasped;
He made vibrating shouts, his first protest against the world's insanity.
    In high, bewildered childish tones, he called home,
But no one was there. I didn't know what to do with him

Any more than one song knows what to do with another—
But sing it! Birds in thorn-thickets have heart enough to chirp!
    He had the fury to demand his needs and a sense of justice.
    How rudimentary freedom is!
The catastrophe of freedom? It escapes! But every barrier's a gate.

    Holly bushes muttered to us: *Wait.* My nephew asked,
Don't you know life? I said, *Not quite. But we're among ourselves.*
And what we know, we know like knowledge in a dream:
Truth lies in secret, like seeds. Forget our links; lose our way!
    On deep, sweet grass in wintertime, he needed more light

Than any day could bring. He shouted at the world: *Come over!*
    He'd saddle up the different moon when she arrived
And brightened up the creek. On flat, rolling landscape, a green rumpled
bedsheet
With a winding row of tile-roofed houses, he would walk hard roads
and smell of moss and rivers.
    When he said *Infinity,* he couldn't see anything.
    He tried to stretch, touch time.
    He answered life, though it was like soothing a bell.

He lay on a pallet like a kindling twig.
We were among ourselves.

Darkness will swallow us in our beds; the atoms in our heads
Will spin apart until we're dead asleep. Before that, music will stroke our
Cheeks. We'll shout near the ocean to God, who is love right through.
Yet, soul of the desert, salt of the sea, this boy speaks
With a voice as sweet as the top string of a lute.

Part IV

Re-Think the World to Life

I see only with my eyes. I love completely, incompletely understand.
   No one can steal what's in my head. I have nothing else.
   My brain doesn't know the difference between what I see and remember.
   I fail to see truth when it sits down beside me. I'm tired of knowing nothing
And being reminded of that, as if an unsolved story were telling itself inside
me,
One that I must guess in the moments it pierces the surface. Then it disappears,
As a dust-speck vanishes the instant a sunray illuminates it.

   I imagine him without him. He speaks pure, unaccented mathematics.
He feels so much truth in his pinky finger, it washes over my face and skin,
Bathes and baptizes me. A student of him, I repeatedly think, over tiny details,
Remember this! Each detail is a curl of yellow sand that holds the ocean at bay.
   'Love'—a dream in its entirety—savors the day's lovely commonness,
The floor, ceiling, air in between; makes 'tomorrow' as ephemeral as his kiss.
I whisper his name—part wish, part blessing. It tugs my heart.

   A few of his brilliant words, and the world's a prism. It reveals that
Intelligence—its weakest blink to the shine of first magnitude stars—is the
same:
A ring of light around a saint's head, and also the math that endowed Greeks
With truth. It's the music behind waves of galaxies and particles alike, the one
Technique of God we share, which my Love has mastered. My first belief will
Be in belief, then in myself, then in him, then in living. He, of whom I think
the world, is a man
Whose peace is a strenuous battle; whose dark is chased by clear and simple
truth.

Confusion overwhelms me: Time seems both to fly forward and to crawl.
Words—*love; life*—move past my mind at all speeds, yet life is slowed by
Thought. The love I speak of with sad awe may be a fantasy built from need.
My thoughts are salt; I try to grasp a fistful, most grains trickle through my
fingers.

    Life never pretended to spare me the effort of thinking logically,
Or the fantasy of knowing everything about him. It's easier to measure
The wind than the intensity of my love for him. And this intensity,
Which my heart produces as oranges produce juice, what does it mean?

    God, who's beyond words, thought Earth into being. Uncertainty doubled;
Tripled; we invented the world of ideas, furnished it with sensations, the
weight
Of idealized love, and meanings that jitterbugged like overheated molecules.

    Truth fell into a thousand fragments in the light of every glance. Life
Split into a daily portion and a secret, interior stream. But dreams are madness;
I'd be glad to know the meaning of the waking world.

Truth can't be reduced to crumbs of information; stale reality on tongues;
Steady rains of lies, mockery and rumors that creep like bad smells through
streets.

    The beast called *truth* can't be caged, though it roams
The halls of justice. It pulls like a tiger at tangled yarns of facts,
To get to the point where each idea and its opposite are equally true—

    Like my Love, who sees opposed forces in will and destiny
Draw toward stunning unity: He and I are one, with all who ever lived.

    We witness oceanic truths and don't know how or why,
Only that they're truths, and smooth space-time fabric's rips.

    Better tell a pail, *Cup the Pacific!* than a mind, *Hold God's drive!*
But our minds re-think the world to life, where every atom suggests
The certainties left when others are lost—perfect passion. Great love.

    In which we walk through doors of space and time
And see we are our meaning.

Sweet Amens

*Very great charm of shadow and light is to be found in the faces of those
who sit in doors of dark houses.*

—Leonardo da Vinci, *Notebooks*

One of my parakeet's feathers dropped near my front door.
   It rose and brushed the ceiling, slanting backwards
Until it fell into the downward current at the back door.
   So, with voices: As they enter the hall, they seem squeezed
From the pressure of artificial light.
   I'm a sparrow, flapping a broken wing, gaining no distance.
   Regret raps its icy knuckles on my head: *Let me in!*

I take a weak breath. My heart beats as if I've climbed a tower.
Sweat dries twice upon my skin.
   Oh, to feel free of all that pulls at me like the gravity
Of two planets! To have that off-the-floor feeling, as if it doesn't matter
What I do! A ball of bright, saffron sun turns the nearby creek purple
And the sky orange—it's the sun, on its way to Africa!
   In a crowded avenue, I notice a face—cheeks and chin

Bluish with whiskers—I recognize. Though I don't speak to him,
He's connected to my memories. It's like seeing a brother
In the face of a cousin. There's an urge to embrace him
Because of our shared measure of blood.
   My heart beats out a high hammer that echoes through my veins.
   Mt feet and arms are a group of drunken wrens. I'm near tears
From fear, the ache between my ears, and the wrenching pull on my neck.

Yet I regret not turning and smiling, making that man let me in.
I can't stand my own company.
My throat's a scorched pipe to a belly full of galvanized nausea
and knowledge: A putrid ball of sap.
Tough it out! Tough it out!
I will my flesh to become more blood and breath, my veins, warmer,
My face—pale from blood that left it—to carry itself as if precious.

But this face feels the air I've squeezed in pull back in my throat:
Fifteen thumbtacks past my Adam's apple.

There are other cousins whom I'm not unlike. Some love me
Fundamentally. There's love I have no choice but to feel for those to whom I
Give myself to devour,
With an urge to nourish, then discard. They renounce me, too, then turn me
Over in their minds. They throw my letters away, unanswered.

I tried to give them settings to shine in. I went out of my way to use nouns

That conjugate, verbs that decline. They study their atlases, come from
elsewhere—
With pale eyes like wood set in wood faces—demanding a path like a plumb-
line.

Vectors are lines with direction and force. We see light, rise to it.
I squint into sunset at relatives walking, back lit, down railroad tracks.
Is it I who, when I tried to hate, veered us off-course?
That's a question so ugly inside me, I'm afraid that if I ask it aloud,
It will grow red-hot claws that twist steel beams to powder.

The very question leaves a dullness in me.
I believe in law and order, which I try to flout.
I'd free myself of all constraints and move, a New Testament visionary,
Through the thorny and gnarled, through the variety of unexpected objects
And events until they shine with their unique nature and I can see parts they
play.
I can't hate. My love is a vector straight out of me into the world:
An ultraviolet ray streaming invisibly from space.

I'm here because my relatives loved.
My brain marches twenty steps ahead of me. I re-collect its odd non-answers.
Negativity's heavy energy seeks something to reduce to nothing—
Like my consciousness. It hangs in mid-air as if it's hit zero-gravity; crashes.
I thought I lived my life. I didn't. It was lived for me,
I came to it, unbelieving. Compassion forced me to believe
That God put perfection here with us—
A shaft of unforced sun through forest roofs.
I drink from my hand, where my heart beats from time out of life
To life out of time, with its waves tipped by apricot-silver. Then comes a despair
From which my insensitive bones can bear anything.
I walk down the stairs, a jerking pencil of light.
My words linger as recklessly as shrouds of silk on a barbed-wire fence.
My consonants may sound like curses, yet they express who I am,

Rushing home in a fine, electric current—feet to brain—which won't stop
Till I's on solid ground and thank the life I've mourned.
In my heart, I was raised by a pair of wild warblers.
They played dumb; lied at top-speed; shouted insults.
They expected me to have a great soul.
Every word they said was wrapped in a mistake.
While furious stars dove into the gray-green sea,

Powerful vectors of heaven headed toward them.
I pressed my parents' wounds so hard, my fingers mended.
From their throats, spilled many sweet amens.

Daredevil World

Time began when a speck of space burst into being from the unknown.

I've been afraid of grief, afraid to read the papers, deaf to even
Simple harmonic motion. An inveterate believer, I latched onto religion
To bolster my gift of fantasy, which is far more important than a talent
For absorbing pig-ignorance.
I've been beaten up until my eyes were ringed. I may be dumber
Than a bag of bugs, but these days, I'm not cautious. Why not play?
Invent reality? I've got a rodeo buckaroo look in my eyes; stars and stripes
On my cowgirl hat. My odds? 100,000 to 1!

My vacant, vain life is only tolerable as an act of rebellion.
I owe it no loyalty. I might as well beat it beating me to the punch.
Why dream some banal dream of kitchen chores and dust pans?
I can dance the side I'm on. Or dance the side I'm not.
I can flash my sewing scissors, threaten *People Magazine*.
Or leap onto my dining table like a tiger with a torch, set fire to dinner.
Gambling is legitimate and not all that unhealthy—we take chances
When screwing in a light bulb!

Why wait? it's the nuclear age! I can continue
My disintegration closer to a Methodist Church, whose door
I'll swing open with my hip. I can drive myself beyond myself!
The possible unification of forces drives me wild.
But if I could, I'd banish all right angles from the universe.
I'd invent new faculties of cognition or discover how films
Might be projected on our eyes and charm away common sense.

Meanwhile, I'll burn rubber in my Chevy and race downtown—
There's a man shrieking at the sleet that cuts his face.
But the number 2 pencils on my desk have joined the word-wide rush
To inanition. My heart slows; the blood sinks softly in my veins.
Deep in the riverbed of my brain, something detaches itself,
Tumbles in the undertow, then rises to the surface like a blackbird
Bursting out of a maple and taking off.
Despite my lack of motion, I gain his strength
And sing in sympathy.

In despairing eyes, I see weather, water, land—alive, opaque, implacable.
Ideas burst in, bamboozle me like flocks of multicolored pigeons.
They give me the illusion of freedom.
I imagine spirits trying to reach me, to enliven my breath
With colors, as extra oxygen brightens fire.
With red sparklers, I write the names of my dead on the sky.
Fireworks pop white noise into the open-throated night.
Here is a person. Here is a person among persons. Here am I,

Who live in this atmosphere like a kitten in a kitchen in a grief-impacted city,
Unaware of the smallness of her time.
I've lived in a world of little mental comforts—helpful fantasies
Like *I write*. Then a vision of my death by mutilation swings in
By idea-trapeze. Time after time, I've refused to go on with my juke-box soul.
I've lived on rotten fruit, greeted the worms in tomatoes.
I've set up instant prisons everywhere I've been.
I speak a few words of personal history; retract.

My doors hang off-center, swing shut by themselves.
One evening, a door jerked open. The night wondered why the day before
Was incomplete in its continued indolence and mindless entertainment:
Families of acrobats in silver tights faded by hurricanes. They had faith
In their impossible tricks, their muscle-bound bodies leapfrogging each other,
Infected with purpose and the otoliths that say, *this way is down!*
Falling is the most natural thing that can happen.
Falling is also a dance.

To live life in the dangerous air! My body remembers how to leap!
Swifts come fast from battlements, dipping and wheeling so high,
They seem flakes of ash. Their wings tip the scale from death to recovery.
Their vaguely human throats sing, *let us live imperfectly!*
A strobe swirls in my brain; my eyes reel and roll. *What now?*
Now what? Escape one pit? Trip into the next? Wring my hands and wail?
Despite backslides before me, watch me—living, breathing, kissing
My illusions as they leave! There's a hole to go through in the daredevil world!

Where Mares Foal in Mid-Air

I've got nothing against the light of day.
I jolt in and out of it. I see colored sparks flying off
My knives and forks when I look from the corners of my eyes.
    Then, I'm conscious of nothing but relief
From my fever so high, the kitchen walls shrink.
    It's been days since my last episode of losing time.

    I'm an Icarus without wings, looking for Daedalus
With my wish to fly to new elsewhere.
    Mist rises from the lagoon outside my picture window
Like steam from a boiling pot. The estuaries are as radiant
As dream dust-motes afloat on a projector beam.
    I move across the kitchen floor like water,

Sing a stave of music like a warbler.
    Since I have the right dreams, a man appears
With open hands. He says, *you can't dream off a fever!*
    His eyes hold x-rays. *Crack!* The windows shattered.
    My left-hand scrapes brick; the right strokes the streaks of leaded glass
That line my front door.

    A sycamore stands sentry at either end, lurid red leaves flaming.
    It sprouts pigeons, parakeets, prayers and pyramids.
    When it speaks to me, we re-invent conversation.
    Since music lives in the leaves of that sycamore, maybe it's also
In the chords which sound in that man's voice.
    He paints the musical scales: Shining gold leaf for the top notes,

Falling through ochres and reds into deep blues and purples.

He's painted my life: A flying swath of silk.

Constable's hundred sketches—'skying'—showed clouds fall away
From Earth, not looking down to where all is confounded.

I find time for visions in my hands: Tiny caribou with twitching tails
And milk-white velvet antlers, gliding through jungles, barely brushing the
Ground;

Rainbow-edged, out-of-focus auks; mares with diamonds woven in their
Manes, foaling in mid-air. I dream of dancers who can't touch ground, then of
a field
Of poppies, transformed to a ballroom. I reconstruct the ballroom,
Make it bigger, dream my entrance to the ballroom,
Dream great dancers, become one.

People look out of their office windows

And see every animal species, running on the breeze—there wasn't room
On the streets. The babies slip out in red bundles, are untucked by their
mothers,
Who breath into them.

I shake and break out in a rash.

A girl skies past me in a top hat.

I take an armful of roses and sweep the floor.

I enchant a bull and rider into the sky,
Then weather-refugees in space arks, sneering at the sun.

The daydreams threaten never to return me to my ambition
To be a parade queen. They veer into hallucinations of extinct narwhals,
Singing, *Welcome to our city, Hallelu!*

The city's scattered with tiled pastel buildings, as if a giant shook them

In a cup and tossed them into the poppies.

A delicate cologne steals in. It's that man's!

He's walked for hours toward me. He' a flowering mimosa;
His face is in its sprays. His trunk leans over me, my labyrinthine, folded
flower.

We embrace in slow motion; in lilac, hydrangea, lavender.
Sleek animals in the sun, we make our bed on the edge of my dream.
When I imagine the universe without him,
his charm enters my dim dimensions; his beauty quadruples.
His voice forms yellow spirals, which wheel as they rise
like lines of stars between collapses, shining with atoms created inside.
His eyes are the color of a lake. He *is* a lake.
His eyes are as transparent as my picture window. He *is* my picture window.

He moves as if he's risen from Elysian Fields.
I cry to be in my reverie with its cloudbursts of hope.
A mare enters twilight sleep to foal; my phantasms keep me in love
with the unseen, where small spoons hang from sycamores.
When I dream no more flying horses, I'll *Sing, Tarry-oh day*
and finally, die, dreaming.

Two Goddesses

I don't believe you can lose people right out of memory.

I passed twelve elms on the mile to school. They stood for family.
In fall, the bare branches jolted chill air, especially against my memory
of countless elms on roads. Seeing so few was to view loneliness.

I recall past scenes, tug each feeling thread. I wish our old house
Were a museum with brass stands and black velvet ropes to block in
Every scene mine and my husband's—like our overgrown back yard.
The little oak beside the house recorded seasons in expanding rings.

I tremble that I might forget the love of him most real: Now, gone. Wisteria
Cascaded down our trellis. Leaves printed shadows on other leaves.
An icy-chill seeps through my picture window here in Florida,
Leaves me tender, bruised, not my solid self but a Tower of Silence.

I wrap tightly, like Mamma's moonstone necklace in a square of lace
From Bruges, the frail feelings in my bones.
I confuse memories of my husband with those of other warm flesh
That's sheathed me. I forget him. Forgetting him, I know him deliberately.

Sense-memories from when we bought our small, Chicago house
overpower me.
To contain our joy, we planted the oak and two Japanese magnolias.
Our life was as lovely-wild as the African violets that filled our backyard,

With the harmony of a finely tuned lute.
I thought I'd have no love left when my husband died, just obey fate

As if written in smoke. Yet I loved those who woke me, even with bad news.
  I'd known people—like my mother—who'd had everything, lost it,

Then made their minds up to hold and be held. Mamma spoke haltingly,
Voice hollow, of the tornado that killed her parents, as if it were a fight
To tear out shards of memory: How the wind chimes on her parents' porch
Rang frantically; how surf frothed their strawberry field. Her father said

To her mother, *Hear the sky?* Theirs was the only house lifted by one twister,
Dashed down by its sister.
  How could air have seized them with such ferocity?
Heaven never warned them of the sudden rivers that bit red Louisiana clay.

God's finger scattered every atom it couldn't de-materialize.
  Memory's a geological cataclysm, shattering all there was.
Yet I put my store, that others place in numbers, in the art of remembering.

  I feel, as many times before, the sun's light curve around the Earth.

  On this rain-scratched Florida day, my breath takes shape, a cobweb
Of air which had been inside me. An unbroken chain of gulls unspools into
A black, wavering thread across the sky, slipping through time's fingers.
Heat, a furnace blast, warps the air.

  Butterflies close their wings in prayer, then flash their black and yellow
Semaphores, past a line of peaks which serrates the sky like a row
Of courtiers bowing and backing away from an emperor.
  A heron races its image over the lagoon.

  In my rose garden, a bowl of earth, I have twin altars:
The goddess of memory, with her defined cheekbones and full lips.
And her sister, Oblivia, the goddess of forgetting, her face rubbed smooth,
Joints as swollen as knobs on a bonsai's branch. Lines pleat her face

And her eyes seem elongated, as if melting. Both smile in reduced gravity.

Past Mnemosyne and Oblivia, I descend to scented pink creepers around
Cypresses. Memory's sun patches shift with breezes.
    Since time was unleashed on us, what's it been but an unceasing wind

That scribbles our news upon itself? Forests blaze; rivers boil; we forget.
The fact that we sometimes fail to recall Oblivia proves her existence.
But there are bits of life I can't lose, since they're knotted into longing that
Rises with the moon. My books' mildew ages the twilight; fills my rooms.

    Memory is an open door in a tornado. It flings my scenes around,
Detached, no before or after. I sift frantically for pieces.
    There's settling, solace in forgetting.
But we can't lose memory: The sudden laughter; the events of troubled Earth.

    Even I won't rest until I have the world written down on paper—
How Earth lay night-long, washed in rain's grace.
    Our errors are the cacophony of untuned horns.
If we lose everything, we'll be fate's lightest loss

    Oblivia looks like an empty hymnal. Mnemosyne's unchanged.
A garden should be paradise, where we walk to words.
I dwell on our backyard of peace, two degrees away by turn of world,
Where I was the magnolia bloom that never fell to Earth.

Hurting Earth

No, not mine: It's somebody else's wound. I could never have born it. So, take
The thing that happened, hide it, stick it in the ground. Whisk the lamps away.

—Anna Akhmatova, "Night"

When I lie next to Earth, I can hear her secrets
Her aura of peace disguises too much pain. Take that peace for granted,
And its pale, cameo perfection shatters.
God's loveliest creations are quiet. They steal unnoticed
Into our lives: Air; sunlight; the sweetness of garlands; banyans
With edible leaves strung with candy-colored lights; wheat fields
Which sweat blood-red poppies; water's glowing molecules,
Lording it over yellow-orange birds of paradise.

In our tiny, brittle craft—hurt Earth—that's navigated the millennia,
There are still rivers of Babylon where we can sit, weep, and speak of Zion.
The slanted sun gives the broken terrain a frozen look; surreal; stupefied.
It knocks my unconscious from its perch. I joined the hurting Earth.
I live with my back to the past; deliver new masks to my unperturbable
God.
The air is as still and expectant as a breath indrawn
With humanity's helplessness to foretell disaster and shield itself.
In hours of my half-sleep, time speeds and bends around planets;

It's made of the same fabric as space, curving like the sea. There's still a
serenity
In water's surface: no ripples; no wind to lean on; only the wonder of stillness.

To the immaculate monotony of long, identical days, still come repeated
Hissings of herons. Doubled willow fronds' reflections rise to meet those
Of falling ones. I see my love's shadow slip from my kitchen to my bedroom.
In my soul, calla lilies burst into bloom.
Psalm twenty-three breathes into me the heart of possibility,
Embodied in the Madonna—guardians of Earth—lifting their skirts
To dance in the dim Spanish churches of Quito and Madrid.
My love has a way of looking that makes me wonder
If he sees from his eyes. Maybe he looks on after everyone else has stopped.
He moves like he's crossing a bridge. He writes of roads that wind forth and back
Against the ruptured skyline of cathedrals, into forests of oak arks;
Into wide fire-gaps which cut through pines toward sawmills; and how,
As we climb, the horizon keeps changing.
He'd have planted persimmon bushes in the desert,

Designed a museum like a peach tree, a capitol city like a bird of paradise.
We've lived plenty long enough to find our way there, not long enough
To forget it. Not long enough to forget we can't be separate from nature's
Waterless aquifers; coral-less reefs; wrecked ocean edges.
My love's clairvoyance bypasses my laggard brain. It gives my soul
A welter of uncertainty, forces us to fashion future selves. The ocean knows
Only how to rise over degraded paradise. Once, I saw the Amazon race
Between my feet,
A multicolored carpet.

Is the future leaving? Terns still dip like swallows as they fly from Svalbard,
Crossing the Atlantic, down the coast of South America
To Antarctica. Glaciers flow downhill toward the iron and nickel core
Of Earth. We have tales as old as time; songs as old as rhyme.
On frozen lakes, ice cracks into polygons.
God hasn't figured things out. Will we?
Moments spill, steeped in my love's heart-chords.
Bright with patient innocence, he scoops up an armful of air.

Noon dips into us. We breathe in music, breathe out exaltation.

Narcotic heaven clings to our arms; we release our thoughts in easy
Breaths, as if nothing had happened here for fifty years except for desert
cinnamon palms
Possessing temperate laurel trees. From the darkening green of a tree of
heaven,
A branch loops over our balcony, scrapes the screen.
    In Quito's Square, light arcs through the monkey puzzle tree:
It bears Earth's hurt. We become what we believe. What do we believe in?
God? Goodness?

    We owe these beliefs to memories trapped like dragonflies
In amber softened by a love of Earth.
    Time is no more fixed than stars. Even Earth's magnetic poles reverse.
    When there's no color left, not even the red of blood;
Not even the white of snow, or a deer's tail; even when we're late,
As if time slipped up on us when we didn't notice,
Earth will spin on her axis: She can't wait
For God's hand to pull ours away from her.

Lord Tomorrow

There are too many examples of men that have been their own
Executioners...some have beat out their brains at the walls of their prison
And some have eaten the fire out of their chimneys...

—John Donne

Each head hears *Gloria in excelsior* in its own tongue.
Each unidentified conspirator owns years of birth and death
Connected by a tiny hyphen: *Life*.
We insist on what we see, touch, know. We think
We live on Earth—as Earth, with her questionable courtesy, deserves.
We're as good at miserably offending her.

We're burdens even to our beds; at fault, for even heat.
Say we're Adam, Eve. Should we be satisfied to probe the convolutions
In our brains from too much thinking what we liked?
Blood flows arrogantly in our veins.
We play coldhearted games, applaud our lack of goals
Beyond our own desires.

My Love and I picture precise paradise:
A sapphire hush of stretched, sunbathing geckos.
Far off, a river crawls. Its yellow surface glints
Over muddy dragon coils.
In history's unpredictability—a bubbling eddy—
There is no arrival.

We're strung against a hot tin sky.
The sun comes down in hallowed strokes: Light into a temple-tree.
Deep trouble rakes our brains, scours our throats
With strokes of comprehension and foreboding flickers.
Recognition that we're threatened is no loss of faith.
Knowledge is formidable and helpless in each rib-cage.

No blind-fool bees, still as praying monks, hover in clouds over our
gardens,
We're in survival-mode. In cut-off towns, dust bears soot
That burns our throats. There's acid in our ginger-ale.
Pollen of the columbines floats upon the air; white light stings our eyes like
limes.
We wanted safety under father-government, who plays Commander
All he can. He's one more conspiracy-nut afraid of death.

He stockpiles food, hoards guns, finances terrorists.
He dares nature, dripping plastic.
Black rings in pink light drift into vision: bubbles in a tank whose fish
drink and drop in shock.

Airplanes circle overhead, atom bombs in holds.
They've veered off-course, correct on faulty compasses.

The Great Bear's geometrical, gives guidance.
Yet days roll over bomb-scapes, rain ash on river currents.
Blood still heats our veins—Lazarus lives for us again.
My Love can see the future through a glass thumbnail:
Wild deer race from sheets of fire. Squalls of parrots shriek
To thirty-feet storm-surges. Flames rip wind like famished beasts tear bones.
We're down a creek, with its plastic carpet on the bottom.
What makes it take two lives to right a wrong?

I hold bad news between clenched teeth and yawn as ugly
As a scream in a Francis Bacon painting.
My love and I still gamble on our bodies—calculating lumps of clay—

And minds—trails of blown, black roses.
  Our illusions are mere rags, stuffed in holes in floors.
  Durga's creativity is balanced on one foot. All her arms reach out.
  She knows we know what's happening!
  We've learned how not to be. Heedless beasts, beseeching God,
We give life logic. Can we *not* defer to executioners, but reclaim the cradle
Of the Nile and Euphrates, where once was born an *always?*
  White ice turns water dark. Oceans drink the sun's reflections,
Warm the air to Arctic fuzz, shut down our brains.
  In cities like once-lovely geishas who've grown ancient, thin,
Abandoned by their lovers, grief's a stealth bomb.
  Babies float—flotsam down a river. Earth opens and the Devil grabs
Some souls through the gashes in between the cobwebs of dry leaves:

An army of dancing wraiths from Hell.
  In *inferno's* forests of despair, wild beasts and fear
Give way to glimpses of a sunlit hill, where no contagion sneaks
Through windows onto our silk bed-sheets.
  Yet madness rises from the Earth in a hot-spring jet.
We're looking into the abyss. The abyss is looking back.

In Full Leaf

Until the dry branch and the shadows fall, I will get me to the hill
Of frankincense complete with spikenard columns and cinnamon,
Myrrh, and cloves, a fountain of gardens...

—Song of Solomon

New shoots swell with innocence, a form of trust,
And peace. Pecans and sweetgums in full leaf
Drench us with their drunken perfume, make our heads ache,
Send orange light drifting from the bottom of our sight—
A smoke-like genie from Arabian nights. It falls into the faintly falling
Universe. A garden, brimful with a dreamy sleep, is clinging to his limbs.

Though I might imagine you and me someplace else,
We've been here all the time—as if in a Cathedral:
On the outside, plain. Inside, it's gold and treasure
    Toward the forest-fringe, young trees are yellow
With new leaves. Woodpeckers drum on trunks.
A birch rises through the dark, ghost-white.

When the sky is purple over shimmering crepe myrtles,
Which toss with a foamy *whoosh*, you and I are drawn to wild terrain,
Odd tongues, strange cultures, mysterious mythologies. Pan was born
In mountains. We might be in Olympus—with open portals,
Painted statues, and 1000 shivering flags, half-asleep in sun so high,
There are no shadows, only the scents of apple trees.

Dogwood blossoms, poised against the heavy air
Of the darkening sky, swim like spots before our eyes in skies
as black as movie houses.
    We've opened the door to a motionless theater—space—
With its silence beyond sound and speech. This domain exists:
It's mine and yours, even with no ever-sweet illusions.

    There's constant music underlying all the other signals.
In the gauzy atmosphere, elusive wings and fins glide through us;
Bedraggled butterflies float drunkenly in hedgerows.
    Dressed in six-foot flowers, buffalo, marabou, impala,
And zebras—with faces like a tribe's tattoos—and elephants—
Using trunks as trumpets—and leopards—partial to baboons—

Wander dreamily. A thousand white monkeys with the faces
Of philosophers and tails like dangling vines, howl riots.
They purse lips into kisses. You and I would kiss them back,
Kiss the flamingoes, who dance, wings spread, in pairs like us.
We'd kiss impalas as they jump and wildebeests who flaunt brittle horns
And fling themselves onto the ground. We'd kiss the reedbucks,

Springing in their great, exultant leaps, laughing in their hearts.
The huge quiet comforts us; we were brought from afar
To witness this array of beasts who know they own the world.
    They browse in breadfruit trees, among acacias. We rub our skin
With tangerines, let goldfish nibble on our fingers like excited Venus flytraps.
    We can't count the colors; we're busy reinventing lovely things.
Heat trembles, wing-like, in the air, to an infinity of cricking katydids.

    I feel their pulses as they live imperfectly, like us,
Knowing no one masters the laws of nature's nature. Here, among
Sycamores and ginkgoes, thorn-trees, plane-trees, Tanzanian jacarandas,
Catalpas, trumpet-creepers, 200-year-old baobabs, 2000-year-old monkey
Puzzle trees—all in an uncomposed harmony—we're set
To leave phenomena and enter the sublime. You and I are transfixed

By the separate beauties, building with the light. In galaxies of beasts
And the flora of God's thought, birth is worth; each hour, holy.
   I give you the love I've withdrawn from everything—except
My chattering parakeets and the cloudberries blooming at our breath.
   For whole moments, we can live within the present tense,
Like saints, loving everything with reverence as if they were emissaries

Of our minds which dreamt them and are dreaming others still.
It's a concerted effort to remind us of all sweetness.
   Mosquitos dream upon our knuckles, make us think
Of what we haven't missed: the harmony we hear in us
And the love we witness in each other.
   In these blooms of paradise,
You, sweet dream, can't end.